JUDO

Other books in the Teach Yourself series

KARATE
INVESTMENT
ORIGAMI
COMPUTER PROGRAMMING

and available in Hodder Paperbacks

Judo

Eric Dominy

London Judo Society
Black Belt Holder and British International

HODDER PAPERBACKS

Printed and bound in Great Britain for
Hodder Paperbacks Ltd,
St. Paul's House, Warwick Lane,
London E.C.4
by Hazell Watson & Viney Ltd,
Aylesbury, Bucks

ISBN 0 340 15072 6

CONTENTS

AUTHOR'S NOTE

I wish to take this opportunity of thanking Peter Johnson (1st Kyo) for the many hours he spent illustrating this book. To his great ability with the pen and brush he has brought a knowledge of judo worthy of a far higher grade. Most of the illustrations are made from photographs of G. W. CHEW (4th Dan), M. SIMPSON (1st Kyo), C. CROSS (1st Dan) and F. INGRAM (1st Kyo) but some are from action photographs taken in International and other contests.

Sincere thanks are also due to the Editor in Chief of the Teach Yourself Books, Mr. Leonard Cutts, who, as well as sponsoring the book, has offered so many helpful suggestions. Without his implicit faith in author and artist *Teach Yourself Judo* would not have come into being.

Finally I wish to impress upon the reader that hard practice and thought are necessary to ensure progress and the final attainment of every judoka's ultimate ambition—that coveted Black Belt, which I hope the teaching given here will help him to attain.

ERIC DOMINY

London Judo Society,
  32, St. Oswald's Place,
    *Kennington Lane, London, S.E.*11.

INTRODUCTION

For many years I strongly believed that personal instruction in judo was essential, until one evening when practising at a very famous club I was asked to look after two beginners who had come down from the North of England. They had been learning from a book and had received no personal tuition whatsoever. Expecting a wasted evening, I reluctantly agreed and, having been introduced, I took them, one at a time, on to the mat, only to be amazed at the progress they had made. As a result, I awarded them both the Yellow Belt of the 5th Kyu grade.

About this time a club was formed in the Midlands amongst complete novices, who had as instructors two men who had attended a week's vocational school, at which I had been present. Today this club is very powerful, having several Black Belts amongst its members.

These stories are told as evidence that judo can be self-taught. It is always advisable to join a reputable club if one exists in your neighbourhood, but it is certainly possible to progress from the book alone. A friend with whom to practise is very much to be recommended, and attendance at any demonstrations given by Black Belts in your area will be of great help. Have a word too with the Black Belts during the interval or after the show; they are always willing to help.

CHAPTER I

ABOUT JUDO

What Is Judo?

The origin of judo is lost in the past. We are told by various authorities that it originated in China, India and Japan, but there is no doubt that, wherever it may have started, it developed in Japan. It is said that in the days of Japanese chivalry it was customary in warfare to refuse any advantage over your opponent. Should one knight be disarmed, his adversary immediately cast away his sword and met him in unarmed combat. This led to training in unarmed combat and slowly a crude and violent but most effective form of jujitsu developed. Professional soldiers opened schools where young Japanese knights were taught how to handle their bows, swords and daggers and also jujitsu. Until late in the 19th century there were many schools of jujitsu in Japan, each with its own master teaching his favourite and specialist tricks. Jujitsu in that period was coming into bad repute; experts having a habit of causing trouble in the bazaars and trying out their skill on innocent members of the public in the resulting riots.

At this time Dr. Jigoro Kano became interested. He studied under many of the old masters and finally devised a system of his own, naming his art, judo—the gentle art. In 1882, he founded the now world famous KODOKWAN School of Judo in Tokio, where judo in its present form was taught. For the first time the more dangerous and uncontrollable moves such as blows were barred, although they are still taught to higher grades, and thus judo could be practised as a sport.

11

Judo is a fighting sport in which hard knocks are both given and received. Don't be deceived by statements that strength is not used in judo—it is. Strength and endurance are required—the point to remember is that the strength must be directed into the exact direction of your opponent's movement. In this form of fighting great use is made of the clothing and in all clubs the traditional costumes which are shown in the illustrations are used.

Although commonly called the art of self-defence, this title is misleading as judo is also an aggressive sport. The locks, holds and throws taught in this book are, I agree, based on self-defence but with the slight modification which all pupils soon learn can be used equally effectively in attack.

In short therefore, what you are about to learn is a hard fighting sport in which every movement has its counter-movement which in turn again can be countered and so on.

Judo was introduced into Britain in 1912 and the foundation stone of European judo was laid by G. Koizumi in 1918 when he founded the first amateur club in Europe, the Budokwai.

Although some very fine judoka, as we call those who practise judo, were produced, judo struggled along in Britain in a small impecunious way until the second Great War, when general interest was aroused by the teaching of unarmed combat in the Forces. In 1946, London Judo Society was founded and for the first time Britain had a second major club. Nowadays London Judo Society has magnificent premises and has produced, under G. W. Chew, generally recognised as one of the leading British instructors, many Black Belts, including three of the youngest ever in Europe.

Why Learn Judo?

Most people who take up judo do so for one of two

reasons; either they wish to be able to defend themselves, or they are attracted by the glamour which, for some reason, attends our sport. They are not, at first, interested in judo from our point of view, that of a sport. After a few weeks they either give up, after finding that they cannot learn to be "masters" in a course of easy lessons, or they see the real possibilities of a sport which has an infinite number of moves each with its counter move.

Judo is a really fine all round exercise, developing a well proportioned, supple body. It teaches self control, and both mental and physical relaxation and balance. Ability to concentrate is increased and judo calls for courage and endurance for, although we get very few injuries, it is a fighting sport. Above all, it develops patience, perseverance and consideration for other people. Thus the exponent of judo develops a philosophy of his own.

How to Learn from "Teach Yourself Judo"

Read right through the book trying to fit the movements described to the illustrations but not studying any individual throw or movement in particular. This will give you a good general idea of judo. Next, commence from lesson 1 and learn how to fall. On no account pass over the "breakfalls," if you are working alone. If you do, you will be a menace to yourself and the members of any club you may visit. Your attention is drawn to the falls again and again as you work through the lessons in order that they may become more proficient as the throws you learn increase in violence. If you have a partner you will soon learn to pay sufficient attention to "breakfalls," as you will be well and truly shaken up if you fail to do so!

Basic principles are stressed throughout, a point missed in so many books. Each lesson covers the main points and then, when these are familiar emphasises the

"Important Points" in a summary at the end of the
description, where you will find some of the finer points
and more important principles listed. Remember that
if you find you require to use strength and force to make
your movement successful your move is incorrect and
will be a failure. If this applies to you, it will pay to
recommence at the beginning of this throw or hold.
Of course if you practise with a "partner" he must
co-operate by placing himself in position for the particular movement to be practised.

Fig. 1.

Each throw or move is described on the assumption that you have such a partner with whom to practise. If not, you will have to try to visualise the moves of an imaginary opponent and check your positions and movements from a mirror—a far more difficult proposition.

A pair of cords or, better still, expander springs attached to firm supports at chest level will be of great help. Do not attach them to a window catch; my club windows are all without catches as a result of this. Tie a loop at the end of each cord and, holding a loop or the handle of the spring in each hand, take up a firm tension. As you turn, pull on the loop or handles in the way described in the lesson on which you are working just as if it were an opponent. This gives you the feel of light opposition (Fig. 1). Springs are better than cords because they are lively and should they pull you off balance as you stretch them with your movement, you know that your throw would have failed or you would have been countered by your imaginary opponent.

This form of practise is advisable even if you have a partner and it is a common sight at London Judo Society to see high grade Black Belts working hard with their judo belts tied to, I regret to say, a window catch.

Difficulties Which May Arise

Remember that some throws or holds may not suit you. A tall man trying a shoulder throw on a much shorter opponent will almost certainly be unsuccessful, but he should not be discouraged. Despite this he should study and practise the throw. The day will come when he either has to teach it to a pupil or may wish to use one of the many variations which will suit him. In such a case, the basic movements will be the same and the reader will regret having neglected the original throws.

Some points of technique are extremely difficult to

describe and understand, even with the assistance of specially prepared illustrations. Readers are therefore advised to turn back every three lessons and revise the moves already studied. You will be amazed how much you appear to have missed and each time you re-read a lesson you will discover new points which will help you.

The main thing is to avoid becoming discouraged. Discouragement affects all judoka at some time or another, mainly because judo is a difficult art. It requires such a small amount of error in timing or direction to cause failure that often only considerable experience and thought will show you the cause of your failure. Always remember that judo is difficult and that only hard and long practice will bring success. If it were easy, it would not be worth learning.

Judo Clothing

As you will see from the diagrams, the clothing worn for judo is peculiar to our sport. It consists of light linen trousers reaching just below the knee and a loose jacket, the sleeves of which reach just below the elbow. It is fastened with a belt which is long enough to go round the body twice and is tied in front with a knot.

This outfit may seem strange at first glance but there are several reasons for its adoption. Judo is based on the idea that if you are attacked your opponent is most unlikely to be naked—he is certain to be clothed in some way or another. Therefore the Japanese used the costume which was usual to them, their native costume.

When in 1918, G. Koizumi formed the first organised judo club in Great Britain—probably in Europe—he saw no reason to westernise the outfit and, in fact, no better one has been devised. The trouser legs and jacket sleeves protect the knees and elbows from unpleasant mat burns—there are no pockets or buttons to injure your fingers and eyes and it is sufficiently loose to be cool and allow full freedom of movement. Above all no form of normal everyday clothes has been found strong enough to stand the great strain involved.

Do not think that it is impossible to learn judo if you are unable to obtain an outfit. Football shorts and an old jacket with pockets and buttons taken off will do, although the jacket will probably not last long. A pyjama cord will do as a belt and no shoes are required as judo exponents always practise in bare feet, as this avoids injuries and in any case is a healthy foot exercise.

The jacket has to be fastened somehow, but as buttons are dangerous a belt is used. A buckle is liable to cause injury and is therefore out of the question, so the belt is made long enough to tie in a knot. It goes round the body twice in order that it may hold the jacket in position more securely. Also the colour of the belt indicates the grade and skill of the wearer. It will be noticed that the colours of the grades progress so that in promotion in grade it is always possible to dye your belt to the next colour without difficulty.

The Grades in Judo

In judo, those who practise are divided into grades according to their skill and experience. These are indicated by the colour of the belt they wear. There are six KYU grades and ten DAN grades. The word KYU means pupil and DAN means degree or master rather like a school where the pupils are KYU's and the masters are DAN's. You will find therefore that when you start you will wear a red belt which indicates no grade but is required to hold the jacket together. Then when you get graded to 6th KYU you will be officially entitled to wear white. You progress through 5th KYU—Yellow, 4th KYU—Orange, 3rd KYU—Green, 2nd KYU—Blue, and 1st KYU—Brown belt holder. You can look on all these grades as pupil grades and then from 1st Kyu you finally receive your degree, the highly coveted Black Belt of 1st DAN, the ultimate ambition of all those who practise judo.

All Dan grades up to and including 5th DAN wear a black belt. From 6th to 9th Dan inclusive a red and white striped belt is worn, but only one European, Paddy O'Neil, has reached 6th Dan so far and he did so after many years practice in Tokio. Tenth Dan is indicated by a red belt which, it has been said, is likely to cause confusion as beginners wear the same colour. As however, in the whole history of judo, the total number of 10th Dans awarded has been three, no confusion appears possible for very many years.

Many clubs give their beginners white belts and on their promotion to the 6th Kyu they retain the same colour. This has the disadvantage of the instructor not being able to pick out the complete beginner and of the beginner himself having no material badge of his first promotion for which he has worked so hard.

Contests and Practise

In all clubs, contests and practices commence and finish with the ceremonial bow, which takes the place of shaking hands in boxing and wrestling or the salutation with the foil in fencing. This bow is, of course, traditional: giving your hand to a judo expert would obviously be asking for trouble. In contests each name is called in turn and the contestant walks on to the mat and sits down in his corner on his heels, his knees on the mat. His opponent takes up a similar posture in the opposite corner when his name is called. They then bow to each other placing their hands on the mats just in front of their knees and lowering their heads sufficiently to show the top of the head to their opponent. Having bowed the contestants move to the centre of the mat and make an attempt to take their holds on their opponent's jacket. As soon as a hold is taken, the timekeeper in a contest, starts his watch. The end of a contest is indicated by the sounding of a gong or the call of 'time,' the contestants returning to their corners and repeating their bow. The formal bow, however, is being discontinued in some clubs.

Should either wish to break off the contest for any reason—usually tightening his belt or adjusting his jacket—he should break clear of his opponent, requesting his opponent to let him do so if necessary, and drop on to one knee. His opponent should immediately adopt the same position and the timekeeper will stop his watch. The contest is renewed when the contestant who required the pause regains his feet. The umpire will only allow this break for a genuine reason and will watch for attempts to use this rule to get out of difficulties or obtain a rest.

Points are won in judo contests in three ways.

(a) A clean throw—throwing one's opponent on to his back.

(b) Forcing him to submit to a strangle or arm lock.

(c) Holding him on his back for 30 seconds.

More detailed explanations are given in the appropriate lessons and in the rules for judo contests on page 187.

CHAPTER II

LESSON 1

Important Note

Throughout this book the word "opponent" has been used to describe the person on whom you practise the various holds, locks and throws. This must not give the impression that you are working against him all the time—co operation is essential.

The Breakfalls

It is essential that before you practise a throw you should be taught the fall applicable to it, especially if you have a partner. Before you commence to practise holds and throws, spend 5 minutes on breakfalls. If you make this an invariable habit there is no reason why you should not spend years at judo without receiving an injury. Some of the falls have been omitted from this lesson as they are dangerous to a complete beginner, but later on, they will cause you no difficulty when practice has made you supple and familiar with basic judo movements.

All falls must be taken with the body curled up and completely relaxed. The arm, or arms, is used as shock absorber and can take about 90 per cent of the impact. If the instructions in this lesson are followed carefully and practised thoroughly there is no reason why falling should cause any difficulty. Experienced judo men derive far more pleasure from taking a well executed and spectacular throw and making a successful breakfall, than they do from making a throw, although you may find this hard to believe at first.

It is quite obvious that, before you can practise the

throws with a partner, the way to fall correctly and harmlessly must be learned thoroughly. At the moment, I will not confuse you with the more complicated methods of falling used by experts for the more violent throws, but will deal with those necessary for the actual throws taught early in this book. As additional methods become necessary, the breakfalls will be explained.

You must have noticed at some time or another, that if you bowl a round object, such as a ball, along the ground, it rolls smoothly and no damage is done. Furthermore, if it is a soft ball, such as a tennis ball, even a bump will not damage it. Now imagine the same thing happening to a square object, a brick for instance. It bounces along the ground all the time knocking lumps out of itself and should it hit a bump it will probably be completely shattered. Now compare your own body with these two examples, the ball and the brick. The average person trips and falls sprawling, with arms and legs flung out and body stiff with surprise—usually he gets hurt. A judo exponent falls like the ball, he relaxes his body to make it soft and pliable, and instinctively curls his body up to take the fall, wherever possible, in a harmless roll.

Take your time over these breakfalls. The main object must be to build up a confidence which cannot be destroyed by a moment's carelessness or over-enthusiasm. Confidence once lost takes quite a time to regain and causes both mental and physical stiffness which results in further unnecessary knocks and bruises.

Breaking Your Fall Backwards

Squat down on your heels, tuck your chin into your chest and roll backwards (Fig. 2). If you roll right over, it does not matter, but it is not necessary. At this stage, you should under no circumstances throw yourself back, just roll slowly and smoothly. The importance of keeping your head well tucked in cannot be em-

Fig. 2

phasised too much, as failure to do so will result in severe headaches and after a heavy fall in your head hitting the floor or mats with unpleasant force.

It is for this reason that all judo falls are taken with the body completely relaxed and curled up, in order to prevent damage to the head, neck and extremities of the spine.

Practise this movement until it is smooth and relaxed, so that you can now proceed with the next part of the breakfall. Lie on your back with your head off the ground and well tucked into your chest and your knees also well drawn up Allow your arms to lie on the ground, at an angle of about 45 degrees from your body, so that the underside of the arms and palm of the hands are in contact with the mats, keeping your fingers together. Now beat the mat with the inside of the arms and the palms of the hands (Fig. 3). This is the part of the arm which is normally against your body if you stand with them hanging limply, palms of the hands against your sides. As you beat the mats, the arms must maintain this 45 degree angle to your body. Keep your arms absolutely

Fig. 3

relaxed, fingers together, and beat from the shoulder. Imagine that you are attempting to flick your hands off your wrists. On no account should the arm be bent or kept stiff as this can result in a painfully skinned or bruised elbow. Once you have the "feel" of the movement, do not be afraid to beat hard, especially if you have a pliable surface on which to practise, proper mats or a thick carpet for instance.

A good example of this beating movement with relaxed arms is a piece of rubber hosepipe. As of course you know, it is limp and pliable, but if you hold it in your hand and slash it down across the ground it looks, as it hits the ground, to be as rigid as an iron bar. This is exactly how you should use your arm, relaxed but stretched out to its full extent, controlled from one end, the shoulder.

Beat with your arms downwards towards your feet keeping the 45 degrees angle. Do not beat sideways. The result, if you keep the correct angle, will be the same but the former is a far easier movement for a beginner to master.

Now you can attempt to combine these two movements but first the reasons for them should be explained. The arm acts as a shock absorber between the body and the floor. It should beat a fraction of a second—when you watch an expert it will appear simultaneous—before your body reaches the ground and this absorbs a good ninety per cent of the shock. If, after practise, you still take a considerable jar, it is obvious that the theory has not been fully understood and you should, once more, work through the instructions paying particular attention to the diagrams.

Once more squat down on your heels as in Fig. 2 on page 22 and, keeping your head well tucked in, roll back, at the same time bringing your arms down in front of you and beating the mats at an angle of 45 degrees to your body. As previously explained, your arms should strike a fraction of a second before your body. When you are thoroughly happy about this and can roll back quite rapidly without jarring your body, especially your spine and neck, straighten your knees a little and roll back from a higher position until you can throw yourself back-

wards when you are standing upright. Figure 4 shows a fall being well taken. For your own good you should on no account hurry your progress and become too ambitious too early.

The Breakfall Sideways

Fig. 4

If you are happy about the backward breakfall, you can continue with the sideways breakfall. The theory is very similar, the body being kept curled up, head tucked in, and the mat beaten with the arm, only this time you lie on your side (Fig. 5). Attempt it on the right side first. You should note that your body must not be fully on the side but half-way between the side and back. For convenience, I shall refer to this position as being on your "side." Lie on your right side allowing your left arm to lie loosely across your body—you will see what actually happens to that left arm later on. Bring your knees up and tuck in your head so that your body is in a "curled

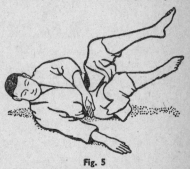

Fig. 5

up" position and beat the mat, still at an angle of 45 degrees from your body, with the right arm. This is how you will break your fall when thrown on your right side.

If you have a good idea of this position and movement, transfer to your left "side." Now the right arm is loosely across your body and you are beating the mats with your left arm.

Next, take up the sideways breakfall position on one "side," say the right for example, and then roll your body over to your left "side" and beat with the left arm. Allow the momentum of your roll to bring your right arm into position across your body. As your left arm "bounces" off the mat let it come across your body and roll over to your right side beating with the right arm. Now roll back to the left side and so on. This rolling movement will give you the "feel" of the breakfall position and assist you to come into it automatically as you will have to do, if you are to avoid unpleasant bumps. It is also a good exercise and will begin to make your body soft and pliable, a very necessary condition for good judo. Control your roll from side to side from your hips. As supple hips are essential to good and effective judo, this is a breakfall and general exercise which cannot be practised too often.

Now you can become a little more ambitious. Squat down on your heels once more and roll to your side. If you roll to the right beat the mats with the right arm, if you roll to the left beat with your left arm—this will give you a very good idea of the sensation of falling and is a test of the effectiveness of your breakfall.

If you have got to this stage and can fall without any undue jar, you can proceed to the next step. Stand upright, feet together, bend your knees slightly, adopting a loose, relaxed position. Now begin to move your right leg across your body from right to left—not forward, keeping your foot along the ground all the way as it moves to your left. Soon you will reach the point where you will lose your balance. When that time arrives allow yourself to fall to your right, breaking that fall with your right arm. Repeat this transferring all the movements to the

Fig. 6

opposite side and gradually increasing the violence of the fall as you become more and more confident and proficient until you can take a fall such as that shown in Fig. 6. Note the right arm raised for the breakfall.

BALANCE

Balance is an essential part of everyday life; without it, movement of any description would be impossible. But because it is to some extent or other instinctive, and does not have to be acquired, people tend to take it very much for granted until the time comes when they wish to learn to skate, or in their youthful days attempt to ride a bicycle for the first time. However even these occasions only incur a momentary difficulty which is soon overcome.

In skating or cycling the actions, as you are using skates or a cycle, are artificial and as you are unused to them it is only to be expected that they will have to be mastered. But in judo, the judo exponent being on foot, the average beginner assumes that, because he can walk or run without difficulty, he should find it easy to move about the mats. To achieve success it is essential to rid oneself of this idea; the art of balancing oneself now assumes new and greater proportions, for not only are you now going to have to balance on one foot but you will have to turn whilst doing so and above all to control an unwilling opponent at the same time.

Posture

The position you adopt on the mat is vitally important to your success in judo. Remember the basis of all judo is summed up as follows:—

"However well you break the balance of your opponent, and however much you have him under control, all is wasted if you are unable to retain your own balance."

It is only through always adopting a correct posture that the necessary state of balance is obtained and continually maintained.

Stand upright on the mat, keeping your feet apart—about the width of your shoulders is ideal—the knees should be bent slightly and the whole body relaxed so that its weight slumps on to the abdomen (Fig. 7). In this way, you will find that a straight line could be drawn up through your toes, knees and abdomen. This is the position you must endeavour to retain however much you move about. At no time when moving should the feet be brought too close together, never closer than about 18 inches, whether moving sideways, backwards or forward.

You should watch your opponent at the level of his eyes or chest, do not look down at his feet which would curve your body too much, leave you open to your opponent's throws and reduce the effects of your own efforts.

Fig. 7

If you have to move to the left, glide your left foot as far as you can with comfort in that direction, keeping your weight evenly balanced and then bring the right foot up to within about 18 inches of it. Practise this slowly, taking several steps one way and then in the reverse direction until you can move about rapidly in either direction without any loss of balance. Do not become discouraged if you cannot "master" this in a few minutes as it takes the judo expert years of constant practice to move freely on the mats with rhythm whilst maintaining excellent balance. Really hard practice at just moving about the mat will be amply repaid because your judo, both defensive and offensive, will improve out of all knowledge.

The foot over which you have the main part of your

weight should move first. In other words do not make a conscious effort to move your foot or leg but move your hip first, the leg of course must follow. All judo movements commence from the hips. It is a fatal mistake to offer your opponent a "loose" foot or leg.

Walking forward is somewhat similar. Glide the right leg forward controlling the movement from the hip and keeping your weight over the hip. When your right foot is firmly on the mats, bring your left leg forward in the same manner. Take care not to bring your left leg too near to your right as it passes and keep the feet about 18 inches, or the width of your shoulders, apart.

These movements must be practised hard and then you can attempt the diagonal movements to the front and, what is even more difficult, moving backwards.

When moving about in a contest, or friendly practice, there is one golden rule you should always observe.

"Never Cross Your Feet."

How to Hold Your Opponent in Judo

In judo there is no compulsory hold that must be taken on your opponent's jacket such as you see in the various forms of wrestling. Years of practice and contest have shown that the best grip is to hold your opponent's left

lapel with your right hand at about the level of your own chest and with your left hand grip your opponent's sleeve just below his right elbow (Fig. 8).

As stated previously, this is not a compulsory hold, but naturally a standard grip is necessary for the purpose of teaching and many years of judo have proved this to be the most effective for a right-handed person. For this reason, therefore,

Fig. 8

all throws taught here will commence from this standard hold although as you progress there is no objection to your varying this to suit your own personal ideas and favourite throws.

All throws will be taught right-handed, which suits this hold. There is, however, no objection to the hand holds being reversed although this suits left-handed throws.

There is a very good reason for this hold. If you experiment you will find that the grip with your left hand below the elbow fully controls his right arm and therefore has the power to break up his attacks before they can develop into throws, also when you make your own attack this position gives you the maximum possible leverage whilst retaining that control over your opponent.

The hold of the right hand on the lapel is used to drive your opponent round in the direction of your attacking movement and again this is the position of the greatest leverage. You will appreciate the importance of the hold later on.

How to Break Your Opponent's Balance to Left and Right

This is without doubt the most difficult part of judo and it will take you many years of practice to become proficient. To attain absolute perfection is impossible in any section of judo, all that one can hope to do is to become as efficient as possible. However this must not discourage you as you will soon learn all that is essential to make self-defence against an opponent who is unpractised in judo most effective should the necessity arise. Similarly a few weeks training will teach you enough to give you considerable fun and exercise from the point of view of judo as a sport.

No doubt at some time or other you have moved a heavy box or piece of furniture and have found that to lift it bodily is impossible. The solution is to tilt it forward or away from you and then on to one corner.

From here it can be rolled on to another corner and so on until it is in the required place.

The human body is very similar to your box in that it stands on a flat base with four corners. These corners are the heels and toes of the feet. If then you treat an opponent in the same manner as the box, you will break his balance. In other words, to break his balance you manœuvre him so that his weight is transferred to his toes or heels, or even better, to the toes or heel of one foot. At this stage the main and most difficult part of the throw has been completed.

A man's balance can be disturbed in any one of eight possible directions; directly to his front or rear, left or right, left or right rear corners or left or right front corners. To break his balance in any of these directions requires different treatment but this will be better studied when individual throws are considered.

In judo, all throws are made in a circular movement. When you and your opponent are holding each other in a normal grip, both your bodies should be curved slightly forward as if a huge ball were between you (Fig. 8) with your bodies curved round it. In all your movements that circle must be kept there. This also can be examined in more detail as I deal with the throws individually.

Taking up the position shown in Fig. 8 and keeping the whole body in one solid unit move your left hip backwards lowering your body by bending your knees slightly at the same time. Your opponent should be pulled in a circular movement to his right front corner up on his toes—he must not be pulled down. Now he is off balance and open to almost any throw to his right front. It is a useful tip to keep your elbows well up and out from your sides in order to obtain a wider circular movement as shown in the illustration, but on no account raise your shoulders. This is vitally important for it is the basic movement in judo. Transfer all the movements to the other side and try again until the result is successful and smooth. Note that a smooth movement is far more necessary than results at this stage and for some considerable time yet.

As you lower your hips and withdraw your hip, the left one if you are breaking your opponent's balance to his right front corner, lift him with an upward movement of your wrists. The forearm should remain in the same position but the wrists, pulse side upward, should lift slightly (see Fig. 9).

Fig. 9

Also as you withdraw the left hip your body should follow the movement. In other words, the hip is used in a combined movement of the body and arms and at the final stage of the movement, just as your opponent is about to fall, your arms should be at the same angle to your body (a 90 degree angle between your chest and arms) as at the commencement.

Similarly, whenever you break an opponent's balance, you must lift him slightly. If you overdo this he will be forced to step in the direction of your move-

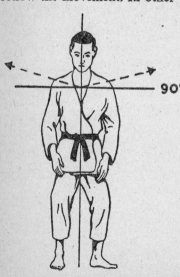

90°

Fig. 10

ment and thus recover himself. All that is required is to bring his weight up on his toes or heels as required.

If you imagine your opponent facing you with a line drawn upwards through the centre of his body (Fig. 10) and another drawn through his shoulders parallel to the ground you will see that there are two 90 degree angles where they cross Whenever you attempt to break his balance you must lift him so that the angle formed by the horizontal line and the line drawn through his body is increased so that it is, however slightly, greater than a right angle (90 degrees). This will bring his weight to his toes and make the final breaking of his balance comparatively easy.

Breaking Your Opponent's Balance to His Front

The basic principles are the same when you wish to break your opponent's balance to his front. Again take up the basic position and use the normal hold shown in Fig. 8 on page 28. Bend your knees and ankles until your knees are well over or in front of your toes; this

enables you to lean your body well backward without losing your balance. At the same time keep that imaginary ball between you by keeping the same relative positions. This is done by lifting him up with an upward and forward movement of the wrist as you lean back. You will find that he comes forward on his toes ready for your throw (Fig. 11) and you will be amazed how far back you can lean without losing your balance.

Fig. 11

Breaking Your Opponent's Balance direct to His Rear

To break your opponent's balance in this direction you must wait until he throws his weight back on, for example,

his right heel. Now turn your left hand—holding his
right sleeve—down into the side of his
body and slightly to his rear, this keeps
him back on his heel and prevents his
recovering or stepping away from you.
With your right hand, keep contact with
his body against his chest or shoulder,
curving your arm forward and down,
forcing him down by turning your
right wrist downward (Fig. 12).

It is essential that your right hand
does not slip over his shoulder, this

Fig. 12

is especially easy to do if his jacket is loose. You must
keep contact on his body. At the same time as you
thrust down with your left hand and curve your right
arm, curve your body forward and step past his right
foot with your left so that your left foot is a few inches
behind his right. Now he should be forced back on
his heels, his body doubled back to his rear, open to
any type of throw in that direction. All these details
are shown in Fig. 12.

CHAPTER III

LESSON 2

Judo Throws—General Principles

In judo one should never use force, but always give way to strength—this is the true theory of judo and the reason for its name—"The Gentle Art."

Imagine for a moment that someone pushes you. Your natural reaction is to push back and in this case either you reach a tiring deadlock or else the stronger man wins. Try this and see what happens. Perhaps all this is obvious so try again, this time allowing your opponent to push you, but instead of pushing back as before draw back your left hip and shoulder pulling him in the same direction as he is pushing. You will find that the lack of opposition makes him lose his balance and with your pull to assist him he will fall past you. Repeat this several times until it becomes a smooth and effective movement. Try again on the other side—to your right and when you are finally satisfied, once more take up the basic position holding your partner's jacket as in Fig. 8 on page 28.

Allow your opponent to attempt to pull you forward to your front. Once more the instinct is to resist by pulling back but don't waste energy in this way—instead go in the direction in which he is already pulling you—and as you do so, break his balance to his rear as you have already practised (Fig. 12), and let his own efforts bring about his downfall.

We have only considered two fundamental actions—the direct pull forward and the direct push to the rear, but these illustrate the whole theory on which judo is based—give way to strength—and allow your opponent to throw himself.

This sums up the theory of judo which is, stated rather crudely, that you help your opponent to continue in the direction in which he is pushing or pulling but rather more rapidly than he wishes. As a result he will lose control of his balance and if you move your body out of his way, usually by means of a movement of your hips, and leave your foot, leg or hip for him to fall over, he will throw himself.

As progress is made and more advanced techniques are attempted it may be found difficult to decide exactly in which direction your opponent's effort is being applied. This problem can only be solved by experience and constant practice. This is a vital point to remember in the art of throwing as it is essential to make your opponent continue in the direction in which he is already travelling and applying force. Whether or not you take your opponent in the correct direction is the difference between success and failure in a throw. At first it will cause you considerable discouragement because one throw will succeed and a dozen apparently identical efforts will fail. Gradually the proportion of successes will increase— only because more and more you allow your opponent to throw himself. Until this judgment develops you will find that you are using strength, first to stop the movement of the opponent and secondly to get him moving in the direction you desire. This obviously requires two actions, both requiring effort, when all that is necessary is one smooth effortless action.

As various throws are taught, every effort will be made to show by means of the text and by diagrams exactly when each throw should be used and in which direction.

It is essential when throwing your partner or opponent to assist his fall otherwise injuries may occur in practice, especially in the early days. Assume that you are about to make a throw to his right—a Drawing Ankle Throw for example. As he begins to fall you must let go of his

jacket with your right hand so that he can breakfall. Hold on with your left hand and lift him up slightly so that he will fall on his back without too much force. As you support him with your left hand bend your knees, keeping your abdomen well forward (Fig. 13). This will enable you to maintain your balance and prevent your falling on him, possibly causing injury. Also, in the case

Fig. 13

of your not obtaining a clean throw, you will find yourself in a strong position to continue with a Hold Down, Strangle Hold or Arm Lock, but I will go into these possibilities later on.

The Drawing Ankle Throw

In nearly all schools and clubs this throw is the first to be taught and this is for many reasons. First because the body movement is the basic one required throughout judo, requiring suppleness, timing and synchronised effort of the whole body. Secondly it demonstrates the art of giving way and allowing your opponent to throw himself. Lastly the technique is comparatively simple—in theory—making it a good and effective throw for beginners.

To simplify all the throws described, I think it best to divide them into parts as follows:—

(a) Breaking an opponent's balance.

(b) The fitting movement for the throw, and

(c) The actual throwing action.

Finally there will be

(d) A summary of the entire throw. This will emphasise

that unless items (*a*), (*b*) and (*c*) are combined into one smooth and united movement the result must end in failure—and, even worse, it will leave you open to a counter throw.

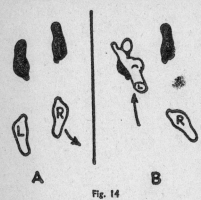

Stand in the fundamental position using the normal hold on your opponent's jacket. Now step diagonally back with your right foot towards your right back corner (Fig. 14) at the same time drawing your opponent along with your hands, your left hand pulling him along in exactly the same arc as that described by his right arm. Your right arm also comes round in the same arc. Here again imagine you are clasping a huge ball to your body with your arms round it. As you step back with your right foot turn it as far to your left as possible and taking your weight with it keep your balance over that right knee (Fig. 15). Now turn to your left on the ball of your right foot bringing your left hip well round and lowering it slightly. Obviously the further round you have turned

Fig. 14

Fig. 15

your right foot in the previous movement the further to the left you will be able to withdraw your left hip. Now in your imagination keep the same hold on that ball and bring it round with you. Thus you see that while your body moves as a compact unit to the left the arms stay in the same relative position only coming round because they are attached to your body.

You will find that as you step back, your opponent must rise on to his toes losing his balance to his right front corner. He can only regain it by stepping forward with his right foot. To prevent this the sole of your left foot should be placed against the front of his right shin, as low down as possible. All that is required is a slight contact which is maintained as you turn to your left by the circular pull of your arms. Your opponent will fall to the mats at your left side. In this movement your right leg should be kept bent but the left leg straight.

Essential Points in the Drawing Ankle Throw

(*a*) Step back with your right foot to your right back corner, turning the foot as far as possible to your left.

(*b*) Pull to your left in a circular movement—do not pull down. Obtain the pull by withdrawing your left hip and not from your arms. Lift him slightly with your wrists.

(*c*) Place the sole of your left foot lightly against your opponents right shin—just using sufficient pressure to prevent him stepping forward. Do not use any pressure as it is impossible to withdraw your left hip if you are forcing forward with the leg.

(*d*) Turn to your left by moving your hip back—lower the hip as you turn by bending your right knee.

(*e*) Remember that all these movements must combine into one continuous smooth action—they are not a series of separate movements. Do not be misled by the fact that they must be described one after another.

Breakfalls

Each time you intend to practise it is essential that you devote a few minutes to your breakfalls. Commence as soon as possible, now if you are reading this in a suitable place, and at once do twelve breakfalls to your left, twelve to your right, and the same number of backward falls. Become a little more ambitious and begin to throw yourself instead of just allowing yourself to roll. Never forget—a few dozen breakfalls before each practice.

Holding Down—General Principles

In judo contests, there are three recognised methods of obtaining a point. The first is by means of a clean throw, the second by means of a "Hold Down," the third by forcing your opponent to submit with which I will deal later. If you are able to hold your opponent down on his back so that you are in full control of one of his limbs and can hold him in that position for thirty seconds without him being able to disturb your hold, you gain a point in a contest. The theory is that, if you can hold him down for half a minute, you can do so indefinitely, and in any case he will usually give you openings for locks or strangles as he struggles.

Theoretically, a hold consists of nothing more than controlling your opponent's body with the weight of your own. You must be relaxed and the only effort necessary is to transfer your balance from point to point as he attempts to escape. Thus, however strenuously he may struggle, you can hold him powerless with practically no effort. An important point to note is that, if correctly applied and maintained, these holds are unbreakable, but often it is possible to bluff the person holding you down into an error. In that case, not only is escape possible but often you can reverse the position.

The Scarf Hold-Down

In dealing with this hold as with the other moves to be described later on, I am going to assume that your opponent is already on his back and is prepared to allow you to apply it to him. Later I will demonstrate how to gain this position in contest work or practice but at present it is essential that you become familiar with the general "feel" of the position.

Sit on the mat close to your opponent's right side by his ribs, placing your right arm under his neck with your hand on the mat by your knee (Fig.

16). Recline on your right hip bringing up your right knee close to his right ear and placing your right leg, from the knee, as far forward as possible. The left leg is thrust back as far as you possibly can with comfort—the leg again

Fig. 16

being thrown back from the knee. Now you are lying in the form of a tripod the three legs of which are your two feet and your right hip. Relax your body against that of your opponent, keeping your weight on your hip and holding his right arm with your own left arm just below his elbow, drawing his arm under your own armpit and holding it firmly between your own arm, thigh and abdomen. It is essential to retain control of this arm under all circumstances—as soon as he is able to free it or disturb your even balance, he will escape without difficulty and in any case your hold is officially regarded as broken.

Practise slipping into this hold until you become completely familiar with it, then allow your opponent to struggle free himself. "Partner" is a better word than "Opponent" at this stage and should be understood throughout when methods of practising are described, as, if progress is to be made, the full co-operation of both "partners" will be required. However, to continue, keep your body completely relaxed—this is not as easy as it sounds—until an effort is made to break the hold. When this occurs, you must drop your weight wherever it may be required to counter the attempt. Should your opponent attempt to move round in order to hook your left leg—the rear one—with one of his legs, you must move round towards his head, always keeping your right knee in the vicinity of his right ear and your legs well apart, and your bodies in the same relative positions as that shown in the illustration (Fig. 16).

Remember that your body is supported by that tripod —the three legs being your right hip and your feet. The more the legs of the tripod are spread apart, the firmer the balance and the more secure the position. However, you must not spread your legs further apart than is comfortable, as to do this makes relaxation and consequently rapid action impossible. Similarly, the nearer the legs come together, the more unstable becomes your position. The object of your opponent when being held will always be to make you bring your legs too close together.

Further details of the hold will be described later as will a few methods of escaping from it.

Arm and Leg Locks—General Principles

If you watch an expert on groundwork in action you will come to the conclusion that judo has dozens of different types of arm locks to be studied; this conclusion is particularly understandable if the expert happens to be practising on you yourself. Fortunately for the beginner this is not altogether true and there are only a few basic types of lock and these can be developed by anyone sufficiently interested so that they may be applied from almost any position, especially against an opponent inferior in skill.

The situation with leg locks is very different. In Britain

they are forbidden because of the particular vulnerability
of the knee and the ankle to injury. Injuries to these
joints may take a considerable time to heal and a damaged
knee can permanently bar the victim from all active
sport. After all, judo is a sport and we do not want to
cause injury to our opponents on the mat and for this
reason every effort is made to ban crude and dangerous
holds and locks. Similarly locks on the wrist are out-
lawed.

Unfortunately, leg locks are allowed in many Con-
tinental countries and are, in any case, together with
wrist locks most effective in self-defence. I propose,
therefore, to include them in later lessons with a note
that they are forbidden by our British judo rules which
are shown at the end of this book.

These locks are usually divided into the following
groups, depending on the particular part of the body
which is being attacked:—

Arm Locks.	*Leg Locks.*
(*a*) The Elbow.	(*a*) The Knee.
(*b*) The Shoulder.	(*b*) The Ankle.
(*c*) The Wrist.	(*c*) Pressure on the muscles
(*d*) Pressure on the	of the leg.
muscles of the arm.	

Attacks on the elbow are by far the most popular,
followed by attacks on the shoulder. The fourth method,
that of applying pressure to, or crushing, the muscles
of the arm is uncommon and very difficult to apply
effectively.

The arm locks are applied against an opponent
either,

(*a*) When your opponent's arm is bent.

(*b*) When his arm is straight.

Attacking a straight arm is fairly easy and a lock can
always be applied, provided you have attained the skill,

whenever your opponent straightens his arm perhaps in an attempt to push you away. As you meet more experienced opposition, you will find a straight arm is seldom offered so that other forms of attack have to be developed. Remember that it is only possible in a book of this size to show the basic type of lock. A great deal of experience and study are required before you acquire the skill necessary to take advantage of the countless opportunities which arise in contests.

It is essential that all locks be released immediately any sign of submission is given and that they are applied steadily without jerks and violence. If this rule is not observed, painful if not serious accidents are likely to occur.

Submission

AS SOON AS A LOCK APPLIED AGAINST YOU COMMENCES TO TAKE EFFECT YOU MUST SUBMIT. Many of the locks and holds can be extremely dangerous and all will cause painful injuries if taken too far. You can also submit if you are being held down and feel that you are unable to break free and that the sacrifice of energy required in a battle to free yourself is not worth while. There is no advantage to be gained in exhausting yourself uselessly in practise but it is up to you to make your own decisions in contests.

In judo, the sign of submission is to tap twice with your hand or foot on your opponent's body, on the mat or on your own body. If, as occasionally happens, you are unable to signal in this way, you should shout. THE MAIN OBJECT IS TO MAKE YOUR SUBMISSION CLEAR TO YOUR OPPONENT WITHOUT DELAY.

As it is not always possible to be certain whether an opponent is submitting or struggling to free himself, it is essential when applying a lock to increase the pressure slowly and steadily and watch for a submission.

At all times it is better to release the lock under the mistaken impression that your opponent has signalled his surrender than to continue and cause an injury. In contests, should you meet an opponent who is stubborn and refuses to submit, it is the duty of the umpire to order you to release the hold and immediately award you a point in order to avoid injury.

The Straight Arm Lock

Throw your opponent with a Drawing Ankle Throw so that he falls at your left side and, as you were taught in the lesson on this throw on page 36, retaining the hold

Fig. 17

on his right sleeve with your left hand and holding his arm up straight so that his right shoulder is lifted slightly off the ground (Fig. 13). This "lift" must be retained until the lock is completed. Now bring your right foot against his body just below his arm-pit and sit down slowly and smoothly against your own right heel. As you do so bring your left foot round his head until you can place your outstretched left leg across his throat (Fig. 17).

You and your opponent should now be lying in the form of a letter 'T' except that your own body must be inclined towards his head (Fig. 18). This enables you to draw his arm down across your right groin. If your body is at right angles to his, his arm will be drawn down between your legs with possibly painful consequences to yourself.

Keeping his arm drawn out to its full extent, pull it towards you and across your right groin, squeezing his

Fig. 18

upper arm hard between your thighs to prevent it from being freed. All that is then required is sufficient pressure from your right hand to hold his arm down and finally the lock is applied by lifting your hips from the ground. Your opponent should be forced to submit immediately.

At all times when applying this lock, and also most others, the thumb of your opponent's hand must be kept upwards in order that the lock is applied against the elbow joint. In other words pressure against the thumb is a certain indication that you are applying the pressure correctly against the elbow. Should he be able to bend his arm with your pressure you will obtain no results for your efforts.

Do not pull his arm down—pull it firmly towards you and apply the pressure to his elbow by lifting your hips.

Keep firm pressure on his upper arm with your thighs. This makes it impossible for him to roll out of your lock.

You must sit as close to your opponent's body as possible If this is not done he will be able to brace his elbow against your thigh. Relax the lock **immediately** on submission.

CHAPTER IV

LESSON 3

The Floating Hip Throw

This is one of the most popular throws in judo. To practice, face your opponent in the normal way but at the moment do not hold his jacket. Step forward with your right foot placing it in front of the right foot of your opponent but **do not** transfer your balance to that right foot. Although you will have to take your left foot off the ground and therefore place your weight on your right, you **must** keep your balance over your **left hip.** Now, still keeping your balance over your left hip, turn on the ball of your right foot and bring your left foot

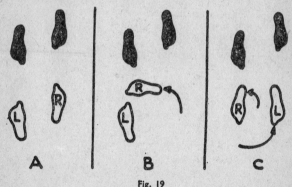

Fig. 19

beside your right, keeping your feet about a foot apart. You should now have your back directly towards your opponent with your feet just in front of, and within, his (Fig. 19).

Try this as many times as is required to make the movement smooth and perfectly balanced. On no account hurry—when satisfied you can do it efficiently, practise it a few dozen times more.

Once more face him and this time take his jacket in the normal hold. Again step in with your right foot, turning it to your left as you do so—this enables your body to make the turn without losing your balance. At the same time lift him with a wrist movement. Now begin to turn to the left and as you do so, release your opponent's lapel with your right hand and allow your arm to slide round his body. Also, as you turn, pull him to his right in a circular movement with your left hand. Do not pull him down, pull him round your body, this will lift him up to his right front corner ready for your throw.

It is essential that your opponent's balance be broken to his front, his right front. In order to ensure this, you must lower your hips, as you move your right foot in, using your wrists to move your opponent on to his toes. Make certain that as you withdraw your left hip, turning your body to your left, your right hand and arm push in exactly the same direction as the pull exerted by your left arm. This applies even when you have your right arm round your opponent's body.

This time when you have com-pleted your turn you should once more have your back to your opponent, your feet just inside his and your right arm round his body holding him as close to your own body as possible. Your knees should be well bent, not only to assist your balance, but also to drop your hips below his—an essential point. At this stage, lean all your weight over to your left. This causes your oppo-

Fig. 20

nent to come right up on his toes so that you can throw him at will (Fig. 20). All that is necessary to complete

the throw is to draw back your left hip and he will fall
to the mats in front of you.

Essential Points in the Floating Hip Throw

(*a*) Step in with your right foot—the knee well bent—
but not transferring your balance to it and at the same
time lifting with your wrists. Just slide the leg in from
the hip, do not move the hip itself in as well. Turn your
right foot as far to your left as possible.

(*b*) As you begin to turn to your left on the ball of
your right foot, allow your right arm to slide round his
body. You must not attempt to force it into position as
to do so will destroy the smoothness of the movement
and, by thus forming a gap between his body and yours,
will make the intended throw a failure.

(*c*) When the turn is completed your feet should be
just in front of those of your opponent and slightly
inside them.

(*d*) Hold your opponent close to your body with
your right arm—close contact must be maintained.
Note that it is dangerous to your wrist and fingers
to hold his belt, although this is very commonly done.

(*e*) From this position transfer all your weight and balance over your left hip in order to destroy his balance finally.

(*f*) Throw him by withdrawing your left hip to your
left—do not attempt to lift your opponent in this throw.

Note.

In practice or contests, it is usually better and certainly
saves an extra movement if, instead of moving in your
right foot as the preliminary movement of the throw,
you move your left hip back at once, passing your left
foot back behind your right and placing it on the mats
beside, but some nine inches away from, your right.

This is only possible if you move from your hip remembering that if you move the hip the leg must follow, but the reverse does not apply.

The 'Figure 4' Lock on the Bent Arm

This is the basic lock used when your opponent's arm is bent at the elbow and takes its name from the position of the arms when it is applied. It can be applied from many positions, but at this stage only the standard lock will be described. You will be able to discover some of the variations by careful experiment on your own.

The opportunity occurs when your opponent lies on his back on the mats and you are able to lie across his chest (Fig. 21). Your body must be completely relaxed with your hips on the mats. It is essential that your opponent's body be kept under your control, as if you fail to do this he will probably be able to throw you off

Fig. 21

or at least escape. Take his left wrist with your left hand and push his arm so that it lies flat on the mat bent at the elbow at an angle either slightly greater or smaller than a right angle. I consider slightly less, as illustrated in Fig. 21, is better but there is often no choice in contests. Bring your right arm under his left shoulder and grasp your own left wrist.

Keep your weight across his chest to control his body and lift your right arm forcing his shoulder upwards. The rest of his arm must be kept flat on the mat. Do not lift up his elbow—concentrate on his shoulder.

To an experienced man it will often be sufficient to

apply the lock with a slight clockwise turn of your right
wrist and forearm, the lift obtained by this turn being
enough to obtain a submission. This method requires
a great deal of practice.

This is an extremely difficult lock to learn and may be
better left until you have done more judo should you find
yourself unsuccessful. Do not be discouraged if this
applies to you as it is common even in clubs with first
class personal tuition.

Essential Points in the 'Figure 4' Arm Lock

(*a*) Control your opponent's body by relaxing your
own.

(*b*) Bring your right arm under his shoulder and obtain
the lock by lifting his shoulder not elbow.

(*c*) Control his arm so that the angle at his elbow
is either greater or less than a right angle.

(*d*) In practice apply the lock gently and steadily and
release it immediately on submission.

In practice make sure that your opponent's right hand
is free to allow him to submit.

Judo Throws—General Principles—2

So far I have described an ankle throw and a hip
throw. Both these are usually made against an opponent
who is tending to push against you and the maximum
effect is obtained by taking him in the direction of his
own effort. If attacked or particularly in judo contests
you will meet the man who keeps you at a distance with
straight stiff arms. This causes great difficulty and will
remain a difficulty to you for a very long time. Stiffness
is especially common in strong, heavy beginners whose
chief concern is to avoid being thrown. This is a des-
tructive and not a progressive habit and is thus very
bad, delaying their own progress considerably.

As a matter of fact it is impossible to make a throw

from this defensive position because to do so you have
to have your opponent at least fairly close to you.
Obviously you cannot do this if you yourself are holding
him well away from you in this form of defence. Even
if you do relax your arms to attack this only gives a
warning which results in a counter. It is the custom in
judo for the instructor to use on his pupil only the
throws, locks or holds which have already been taught.
As a result he is often in the position of not being able
to throw his pupil if this form of defence is adopted.
Do not let this deceive you because you are often open
to some very severe throws which for your sake your
instructor will not use. The time will come when your
progress ceases and you are overtaken in skill and grade
by much lighter and smaller judoka with possibly less
than your experience. These judoka now reap the
benefit of their lack of size and strength which has
forced them to adopt skill from the first. If you are small,
let this encourage you as you will be defeated time
after time in the early stages by less skilful but more
powerful opponents.

How is the problem of this type of opponent to be
solved? The first step to be taken is to make the two
bodies, your own and that of your opponent, into one
solid unit. This is achieved by keeping his arms in
position in close contact with your body, usually by an
upward or inward turn of your wrists. Now step diagonally backwards with your right foot as in the Drawing
Ankle Throw (Fig. 14, on page 37), keeping your
weight and balance over it all the time, and turning
it as far to your left as possible. As you do so, if you
maintain contact, your opponent will rise on his toes
to his right front corner. At this point, if he is held in this
off balance position, he is easy to throw (Fig. 9 on page 31).

An alternative method of disturbing his balance to
his right front corner is to step back with your left foot,

taking it behind your right and placing it outside and to the left of his left foot so that your left toes point in the same direction as those of your opponent. You will see where your feet should be if you look at Fig. 22 which illustrates the Body Drop Throw, this being a throw requiring this method of breaking your opponent's balance. Once more keep your weight and balance over your left hip as you move your left leg and keep the hip travelling in a circular movement to your left. Your arms must also move in this circular movement—not downwards. In this position, no weight whatsoever should be on your right foot once your left foot has been replaced on the mats.

The Body Drop Throw

A very useful throw, the Body Drop owes its popularity to the fact that with only slight modification it can be used against an opponent who is travelling in any direction except backwards. Also it combines very effectively with several other throws and can be used as a counter. Probably its greatest value is its effectiveness against opponents holding you strongly at arms' length, a defence which makes the use of throws requiring close contact very difficult, if not impossible.

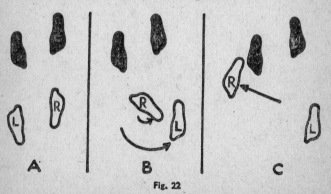

Fig. 22

The opportunity to attempt this throw arises when your opponent holds you with stiff arms and steps forward with his right foot. As he does so, draw him forward with your left arm, causing him to overstride slightly and thus place his weight too far forward over his right foot. At the same time, as you draw him forward, bring your left foot round behind you, crossing it behind your right foot and placing it beside and outside his left foot (Fig. 22 shows the movements of your feet), lowering your hip by bending your left knee as you do so. You must also lift him with your wrists. Bring your left hip back with your leg, at the same time turning your body completely to the left and transferring your weight and balance absolutely to your left leg. Shift your right foot slightly if necessary so that it contacts his right shin lightly (Fig. 23), thus preventing him advancing any further to retain his balance. As you turn you must take your opponent with you by a circular movement of your arms. Do not pull him down—take him round your body, the actual throwing action being the dropping or lowering of your left hip as you turn. Continue turning until he actually falls to the mats.

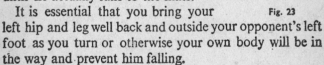

Fig. 23

It is essential that you bring your left hip and leg well back and outside your opponent's left foot as you turn or otherwise your own body will be in the way and prevent him falling.

Essential Points in the Body Drop Throw

(a) Bring your left foot back until it is outside—and beside—your opponent's left foot. As you do so bring your left hip back with it. Lower your hip. Break his balance forward by means of a slight upward turn of your wrists.

(*b*) As you move your left hip back bring him round with you by means of a circular pull and pushing movement of the arms—pull with the left hand and push with the right. The push must directly follow the direction of the pull, it must not push him backward. Imagine that you are attempting to punch your opponent with a right hook aimed at his jaw but keep contact with his body by means of your hold on his jacket all the time.

(*c*) You must bend the left knee in order to lower your left hip, thus placing your hips below those of your opponent. That is to say your hips must be lowered below your opponent's point of balance.

(*d*) Your right foot must contact your opponent's right shin firmly and firm contact must be maintained here in order to prevent him stepping over your foot and leg and thus escaping the throw. You should press back with the back of your leg at the achilles tendon.

(*e*) Finally throw him to the mats by continuing the turning movement to the left with your left hip.

CHAPTER V

LESSON 4

Strangle and Choke Locks—General Principles—1

As in the case of arm locks if you watch a judo expert in action you will see what appears to be a countless number of submissions obtained by means of attacks on the neck and throat. In actual practice, there are only two basic locks and all the others are variations of them. It is only these variations which enable the locks to be applied from what looks like any position.

The more simple of the two is merely an ordinary choke caused by pressure on the front of the throat. This is very easy in theory but not popular amongst experienced judo men because it is not only crude but also very difficult to apply against anyone except a novice.

The second lock calls for more science and stops the flow of blood to the brain by pressure on the carotid arteries at the side of the neck. As in the case of arm locks, these strangle holds can be extremely dangerous and the signal of submission must be instantly acknowledged by releasing the grip. Applied correctly, this type of lock will render a victim unconscious in about five seconds and can do so without the infliction of any pain.

The Naked Strangle

As the name implies this lock can be applied against a naked opponent as no use is made of the jacket. The ideal occasion to attempt this lock is when you find yourself kneeling behind your opponent. Immediately place your left arm round his neck and grip your own right arm just below the elbow. Your left elbow should be placed by your opponent's left shoulder with your right hand pressing against the back of his head. (Fig. 24 should make

this position, which sounds rather complicated, quite clear). Apply the lock by using your arms like a pair of scissors. Pull back with your left arm and push the top of his head forward with your right hand. If the lock is applied correctly with the sharp inside of the left forearm—that part extending about three inches above the wrist joint—an almost in-

Fig. 24

stantaneous submission will be obtained.

Essential Points in the Naked Strangle Hold

(a) Your opponent's balance must be broken to his rear. Place your left arm round his neck and pull him backwards. This can be carried out more easily by pushing him in the small of the back with your free right hand. When his posture is broken keep him in this position whilst you place your right hand behind his head and clasp your right elbow with your left hand to apply the lock.

(b) Use the sharp 'boney' edge of your left forearm against his throat and pull back with your left arm and push forward with your right hand against his head— thus your arms are acting like a pair of scissors which close on his neck.

Straight Arm Lock from an Astride Position

This is another method of applying an arm lock against an opponent who attempts to push you away with a stiff arm. The lock is used when you sit astride your opponent with your weight resting on your heels as shown in Fig. 28 on page 62. This position is very common in judo ground-work. No doubt from here you will attempt to strangle him into submission and he in defence may push against your face, chest or shoulders. At once grasp his wrist very firmly and pull his arm out straight in exactly the direction in which he is pushing. As you straighten his arm, slide your foot forward until the leg is thrust straight out beside his body and push his arm down across your knee or thigh (Fig. 25). The exact position depends on your own personal comfort, bearing in mind that you must maintain

Fig. 25

your balance. The thumb of his hand must be kept uppermost as usual, the pressure being applied against his thumb to ensure that it is brought to bear against his elbow joint correctly.

Essential Points in applying a Straight Arm Lock from the Astride Position

(a) Grasp the wrist of the arm with which you are being pushed and pull his arm straight keeping it so. At the same time you must

(b) Slide your leg forward and pull his arm down across it. Use your right leg to attack his left arm and your left to attack his right.

Later you will find that you will be able to bluff an opponent into pushing you away in this manner by various means such as attempting to obtain a strangle hold.

The Shoulder Throw

This is a spectacular and rather dangerous throw which requires care, especially at first, before you have absorbed some of the finer points of judo which enable the most violent of throws to be made in perfect safety.

In an actual fight, it is a throw used against anyone who aims a straight right at you or who pushes against your body at about shoulder level. In judo, from the sport point of view, it can be used either against an opponent who is pushing your shoulder or keeps his arm stiff in defence. Of course you can and usually must, make your own opening.

To make the throw to your left, wait until your opponent pushes you with his right arm. Pull your opponent forward with your left hand and step in with your right foot placing it just to the left (your opponent's left) but in front of his right foot Fig. 19. Bend the knees and, as in the

Fig. 26

Hip Throw, only advance your leg from the hip, do not bring your hips or body forward as well. Turn your right foot as far to the left as possible and simultaneously curve your body forward slightly, lifting him slightly with your wrists as you do so in order to break his balance to his front. This also is similar to the Hip Throw action. As you slide your right foot in, maintain this lift with your hands, in order to bring him on his toes. Now turn to your left on the ball of your right foot bringing your left foot back beside your right but keeping them about a foot apart. This leaves you with your back directly towards your opponent (Fig. 26). Your knees should be well bent in order to bring your hips below his. This will ensure that your attack will be below his point of balance and gain maximum effect. As you turn to your left you must pull your opponent hard with your left hand pulling his right arm in exactly the direction in which he is pushing and slightly upwards in order to keep him well off balance and

at the same time retaining your own. Continue this pull
and lift and, as you turn, let go of his jacket with your
right hand and bring your arm under his right arm-pit,
gripping his right upper arm between your own upper
arm and forearm. Do not relax this right hand hold until
he is off balance and ensure that the pull with the left
is maintained as you do so. Don't worry about gripping
with your right hand, just wind your arm round his. Fig.
26 should make this position quite clear. Continue this
pull forward and upward and force your hips smoothly and
steadily backwards in order to drive your opponent off his
feet. Finally, to make the throw, draw your left hip back
and continue the pull and lift of his arm just as if you were
dumping a sack of coal. He will fall to the mats in front
of you.

This can be a heavy throw—you must take care to
retain your own balance and check your opponent's fall
each time the throw is practiced. Even in contest you will
find that experienced judoka take this precaution, even
to the extent of losing a point for a clean throw.

Essential Points in the Shoulder Throw

(*a*) Pull your opponent off balance with your left arm
as he pushes and step in with your right foot bending
your knees well so that you are under him and turn your
right foot as far to the left as possible—this will enable
you to maintain your own balance as you turn your body.

(*b*) Curve your body slightly forward as you advance
your right foot in the preliminary movement.

(*c*) Turn on the ball of your right foot to your left
keeping your body low and curved slightly forward—lift
and pull your opponents right arm in the direction in
which it is already pointing in order to break his balance
and to prevent him pulling you backwards and strangling
you as you will find is done frequently in your early days

of practice. It is essential that the pull with your left arm is continued in the exact direction in which your opponent's right arm is pointing and pushing.

(*d*) Still keeping your body curved forward and maintaining the pull on his right arm push your hips backwards into him. He should be driven clear of the mats without any strength being required on your part. Push your hips back into him—do not lift him up.

(*e*) Finally just flick him off your hips by pulling your left hip back. He will then fall into the mats in front of you.

(*f*) Take care to check him as he falls with your own body upright and hips thrust forward. This will ensure that unduly hard knocks or falls are avoided.

CHAPTER VI

LESSON 5

The Normal Cross Strangle Hold

You have already practised the Naked Strangle, how to strangle your opponent without the use of his jacket. The Normal Cross Hold takes advantage of the clothing. The opportunity arises when your opponent lies on his back on the mats with you astride him. Slide your right hand, palm upwards, under his right collar as deep down as possible. Now bring your left hand also palm upward across and under his left collar, also as deep as you are able. Your fingers should now be inside his collar, backs of the hands against his skin and your thumbs outside his

jacket (see Fig. 27). The sharp "cutting edge" of the inside of your wrists—the same side as your thumbs—must be applied to his neck as deep as possible (Fig 28). Next press your wrists inwards so as to obtain firm but not undue pressure against the side of his neck. Finally, slide your hands towards you

Fig. 27

maintaining the pressure against his neck constantly. Any relaxation of this pressure will in almost all cases mean that you will fail to obtain successful results, especially against a hardened exponent of judo.

The reason this pressure must be maintained as you slide your hands forward is that this action moves the muscles normally protecting the carotid arteries which carry the flow of blood to the brain. It is these arteries which you are now about to attack. Lower your body on to that of your opponent, at the same time leaning forward

and allowing your elbows to pass outside your body (Fig. 28). This makes your arms act once more like a pair of scissors tightening the pressure on

Fig. 28

the neck just below the ears. If necessary lower your body, which must be completely relaxed, until your head touches the mats above his head.

It is essential to keep your body and arms relaxed in this strangle hold, otherwise your rigid arms will not be able to maintain pressure on the arteries as your opponent stiffens his neck muscles in resistance against you. If the arms and body are relaxed the arms will be found to "fit" into his neck and render his efforts at resistance ineffective.

Notes on the Normal Cross Strangle Hold

This lock applied correctly is extremely effective and causes unconsciousness in a very few seconds and when applied by experts is completely painless. For this latter reason you should take care in case your opponent should not realise he is in danger of becoming unconscious until it is too late to submit.

When you attempt this hold in practice on no account use any force and see that your opponent does not resist you too long. Similarly, when the lock is attempted on you, do not be ashamed or too proud to submit as soon as you feel the lock beginning to become effective.

Should your opponent have to submit because of pain on the neck muscles, choking, or pain due to pressure on the throat the lock must be considered to be a failure and is incorrectly applied. Study the diagrams most carefully and once more start from the beginning.

In this lock and the Adverse Cross which follows you must maintain control of your opponent's body. A popular method of doing this is to press your legs firmly against the sides of his body (Fig. 28). Should he attempt to roll you off, which is sometimes to your advantage as will be explained later, you can if properly relaxed push out the

Fig. 29

appropriate leg and so maintain command of the situation (Fig. 29). Note how the thrust against the mat is obtained from the toes and not the side of the foot, this is an important part of groundwork. Of course when attempting a strangle hold you should not release the hold on his jacket.

The Adverse or Half Cross Strangle Hold

In appearance, this strangle hold is very similar to the Normal Cross which you have already practised but unfortunately theory is not always easily effected and in "randori" which is free practice you never find an opponent who is willing to lie passively on his back on the mats while you feel for position and apply that hold. Frequently you will find it extremely difficult, if not impossible, to obtain a sufficiently deep hold on his collar with your hands. What is the solution to this difficulty?

It is usually fairly easy to get one hand in on his collar, so I will assume you have managed to take a deep hold with your right hand similar to that shown for the Normal Cross, deep on the right side of the collar, palm of the hand up, with fingers on the inside of the collar and the thumb on the outside to make the grip secure. This time the hold obtained by the left hand is different—slide it down the left side of your opponent's collar as far as possible—the deeper it goes the better—palm down

outside the jacket and the thumb inside the collar to
obtain the grip. Your left arm, or in case you may be
attempting the hold the other way round, the hand taking
the reverse grip, is always placed above that taking the
"palm-up" hold. The pressure against the neck must be
obtained and the hands then slide towards you to dis-
place the protective neck muscles. Finally lean forward,
lowering your body over his, allowing your elbows to
come outside your own body in order to apply the hold.
Release the hold immediately he submits.

Strangle and Choke Locks—General Principles—2

When attempting to apply any strangle hold always
bring your opponent's neck as close to your own chest as
possible. By this it is not intended that you should on all
occasions when you use a strangle hold make a violent
effort to drag your opponent's neck down on to your
chest. Should you do this blindly it usually means that
your body is stiffened and either the hold is a failure or,
as is almost certain to occur, you will find yourself thrown
off and the positions reversed.

Very often it is best to move your own body so that the
desired positions may be obtained without effort. After
all it is far easier to move your own body than that of your
opponent probably against very strenuous opposition. A
good example of this is the method adopted in the Normal
and Adverse Cross Holds in which you lower your relaxed
body on to that of your opponent in order to gain the full
effect of the lock.

Frequently in judo you have the choice as already
stated of moving your own body practically without
effort or mustering your strength and energy, even should
you be sufficiently strong, to move that of your opponent.
It is obvious also, that whilst you can attempt to move
your own body at will and can usually succeed, your
opponent will always resist your efforts to move him.

Next time you practice "Groundwork" try instead of moving your opponent when he is on top of you just pushing his hips to make a gap between you and sliding your own body away from underneath him.

Counter Attacks—General Principles—1

It must be stressed at once that the secret of successful counters is to avoid your opponent's effort and then assist him to travel in the direction in which he is already moving in his attempt to throw you. The same applies to locks and holds on the ground. **Never resist an opponent's efforts BY USING FORCE.**

It is a very common error, especially with beginners, to resist an opponent's movement and then by sheer force move him in a different direction. This is basically wrong for, however strong you may be and however successful these methods have been in the past, in judo you are certain to meet the experienced opponent who will turn your own misused strength against you with the result that some extremely heavy falls will be taken until this dangerous, and completely futile, habit is broken. An excellent example of the effortless success that can be obtained by giving way is to be seen in the counter to the Drawing Ankle Throw.

The Counter to the Drawing Ankle Throw

When you are the victim of this counter you are amazed by its simplicity and effectiveness.

As usual the counter will be broken up into several movements, but it is extremely important to stress the fact that this is only done to simplify the instruction and when practising the counter itself these moves must blend into one smooth and rhythmic whole if success is to be obtained.

In the first movement forget the idea of counter-throwing and concentrate only on avoiding the throw.

All beginners, when an attempt is made to throw them to their front, push forward with their arms and get their legs as far away from their opponent as they possibly can.

Fig. 30

This certainly will avoid an Ankle Throw but leaves them open to large variety of far more violent attacks of which the Stomach Throw is only one example. To avoid the Drawing Ankle Throw correctly and safely all that is required is to keep your body upright and lift up your right leg, thus allowing your opponent's leg to move harmlessly past (Fig. 30). Taking the normal hold on your opponent wait for him to attack your right ankle and immediately avoid this effort by lifting your right leg. On no account should you move the thigh back as this would throw your balance forward—a position of great weakness. Practice this move until you automatically react correctly. For until it is correct and instinctive you have little chance of avoiding any opponent's throw and even less of applying a counter.

Having reached the stage where you can sometimes even anticipate your opponent's intentions—you will find this possible with experience, and the time actually comes after many years of practice—you will sense his movements so that the counter commences almost before he knows what throw he is about to attempt himself. He moves his left hip back to attempt an Ankle Throw, you lift your right leg and, as soon as his foot has passed, you follow his left foot with your right and apply an Ankle Throw of your own against it. Not only will you catch him standing on one leg but his own movement, especially if it is good, will take him a circular direction and you will find that he is already travelling in exactly the direction as that in which you make your counter throw.

There are several counters to this type of throw but this is the most commonly used and certainly the most simple to practice in the early stages.

CHAPTER VII

LESSON 6

Straight Arm Lock from Underneath

In hand to hand combat the person underneath is generally regarded as being in a very perilous if not hopeless position, but in judo this is certainly not so especially when you learn to move freely and correctly.

You have already practiced a few arm locks but so far they have all been applied from the so-called "position of advantage"—on top. You are now to be shown that very often the underneath position is the stronger. In a general practice you have been pulled to the mats, not cleanly thrown, by your opponent who follows you down If you defend correctly with your legs and elbow, your opponent will almost certainly finish up in a kneeling position between your legs or at least you can prevent him sitting astride you. (This will be covered later.) The opening for this lock occurs when he kneels between your legs with the alternative of either attacking your throat or obtaining a position of greater advantage which is none too easy against an experienced opponent. This position is very common in judo contests and practice and is, to all appearances very much in favour of the person on top.

From this uppermost position there are three possible methods of attacks, the first two incidentally useless from between the legs if attempted against an experienced man.

(a) An attempt to apply a strangle hold.

(b) An arm lock, usually the Figure Four variety and

(c) To change the position.

Very few people except experts have the moral courage to change the position as they feel safe as they have their opponent apparently helpless. An arm lock proves difficult as one has to reach right forward in order to get the balance right over the arm to be attacked, it is really too far away, and in any case it is basically bad judo to attempt a lock without having control of your opponent's body, and you certainly haven't got it from this position. Finally, almost inevitably, the first alternative is adopted—an attack on the throat.

As your opponent kneels between your legs reaching for your throat (Fig. 31) immediately take a firm grip on his right wrist with both hands if pos-

Fig. 31

sible and bring your right foot up into his left groin or against his left thigh (Fig. 32). Straighten your leg thus straightening his body leaving him stretched out with his

Fig. 32

right arm, if you are maintaining a firm grip on his wrist, straight out along your body. Now roll slightly to your right, bringing your left leg right over his right arm above the elbow

Fig. 33

and passing it underneath his head (Fig. 33). Move his arm steadily upwards pressing down with your leg. Release the lock as soon as he submits. At first only try this lock slowly and smoothly on your opponent who should not for his own sake resist. Neither should you when it is your turn. All arm locks in which pressure from the leg is applied are particularly dangerous as the leg is not so sensitive to tension as your hand or arm nor so easily controlled.

Essential Points in the Straight Arm Lock from Underneath

(a) Ensure that if you use the right foot to straighten your opponent's body you grasp his right wrist. This is not as easy to carry out instinctively as it sounds especially if it is a strangle involving crossed hands which is being attempted on you.

(b) A simultaneous action of the hands, foot against the groin, and the opposite leg to apply the lock are essential to success. If you move your right leg first, your opponent will roll you over and obtain a lock or hold on you in an instant. If you bring your left leg over his body and arm too late, he'll avoid the intended lock and escape under your leg. You can try this—carefully—for yourself and discover its possibilities. If you grasp his wrist too early, your opponent will anticipate your idea and once again it will become ineffective.

(c) The lock can of course be carried out equally successfully the reverse way with all the movements carried out with the opposite hand and foot and should be practised that way.

(d) As in all judo movements, the simultaneous and controlled actions of the whole body combine to give a smooth and effective result.

The Major Outer Reaping

This is one of the most effective and popular throws in judo. For the first time you are going to practise a throw which is carried out in self-defence when your opponent pulls you and when practising judo as a sport as your opponent is moving to his rear. The possible danger arises from the very real chance that the person taking the fall may strike his head on the mats. A revision of the backward breakfall prior to practising this throw is therefore very strongly advised.

As usual take a normal hold on your opponent's jacket and wait for him to place his weight on his right foot. As he does so, take a long gliding step forward with your left foot so that you place your foot beside his right (Fig. 12 on page 33). Even step past his right foot if you can. At the same time, curve your body forward so that all your weight and balance are over your left foot and hip. This is also illustrated in Fig. 12. Simultaneously with stepping in and curving your body forward you must break your opponent's balance. This is effected with a movement which is difficult to describe. As you step in with your left foot you should lift your opponent by turning your wrists upwards and then, as your left foot is placed on the ground, the wrists turn down so that a circular movement has been effected, the movement commencing about

level with his chest, raising as he is lifted with the wrists and then dropping again as the wrists turn down. His balance is finally destroyed by continuing the downward turn of the wrists, the left arm being straightened downwards so that his right elbow is forced towards the ground slightly to the rear of his hip. Your fist should be turned towards the ground as if you were about to punch the mats. Your right arm is also straight-

Fig. 34

ened but this time you should force him downward with your right hand by bending your right wrist down, thus obtaining downward pressure against his chest or shoulder depending on where you hold (Fig. 34). These movements not only prevent your opponent stepping backwards into safety by forcing his weight on to his heels but also double him over backwards so that you can throw him by merely continuing the movement without any attack with your legs.

Finally—note that all these movements must become one smooth flowing whole—when you have your opponent bent over backwards in a helpless position, bring your right hip forward placing your leg so that the back of your thigh is against the back of his right thigh and sweep your leg back from the hip curving your body forward as you do so. By this means, the whole of the strength and power of your body is used in the throw. Your opponent's legs will be swept completely away from him and he will fall heavily to the mat on his back. On no account should you kick your leg backwards or you risk painful injury to the person being attacked and yourself; it must be a smooth continuous thrust, the effect being obtained by the combined actions of your hips, leg and arms. His fall should be checked with your left hand in the usual way.

Essential Points in the Major Outer Reaping Throw

(a) Glide your left foot well forward curving your body forward in order that your balance is completely over your foot. The further past him you move your left foot, the more effective the throw becomes and the less likelihood there will be of a counter attack. Ensure that the body curves forward with the first movement so that your balance remains over your left hip throughout. At the same time, lift him slightly.

(b) As you bring your left foot to the ground, straighten your left arm towards the ground and curve your right arm pressing your opponent down with your right hand. This will force his balance back over his heels and prevent him avoiding the throw by stepping backwards away from you.

(c) Bring your right leg forward from the hip and sweep it back against the back of your opponent's thigh.

Variation to the Major Outer Reaping

It is possible to vary the method of breaking your opponent's balance and this enables the throw to be made when your opponent is advancing as well as retiring. This time lift him with your wrists, the wrist being turned downwards like the neck of a swan and bring them in towards you until you have close contact, his chest being close to yours. Now bring your right hip past his right and reap his leg away as already described. As you do so, break his balance backwards and downwards as in the previous method.

The Upper Four Quarters Hold Down

There are probably more variations which are fundamentally sound to this hold than to any other movement in judo. The method shown here is the basic one and is that usually taught. It is also the most easily applied.

The opportunities to apply this hold arise when your opponent lies on his back on the mats. The object of this lock is to pin the upper part of his body; hence its name. In order to do this, place your body on his with your chest on his head and tuck your own head firmly against his

Fig. 35

lower chest. This is essential to protect your head and neck as there is a danger of a neck lock counter to this hold. Your legs should be thrust out behind you, well spread out and with your hips lowered on to the mats—your toes should also be dug firmly into the mats (Fig 35). It must be left for the illustration to make this position quite clear as description is extremely difficult and confusing. Your elbows should be dug deeply into his arm-pits and your hand should grip his belt at his sides. If this position is maintained your opponent will be deprived of the use of his own arms and will find escape very difficult. On no account support your weight on your knees as to do so will certainly result in your being thrown off without delay. Experience will give you the "feel" of this position and enable you to know when it is correct or otherwise. Your hips should be slumped on to the mats and your body, completely relaxed, resting on your opponent. It is essential to maintain the same relative position to your opponent as he commences to struggle to free himself. As he moves round to right or left move your body in that direction as well, if he attempts to lift his left shoulder exert pressure on it by pressing with the toes of your right foot on the mat and take this action with your left foot if he tries to lift his right shoulder. An attempt to sit up should be countered with even pressure from the toes of both feet pressing down with your head. If you keep your legs well apart and your body in a straight line with his, you will retain full command but you must remain completely relaxed as your reaction will be too slow if there is any stiffness. Your hips must remain on the mats all the time however you move.

Essential Points in the Upper Four Quarter Hold

(a) Hold your arms well into your opponent's body thus making it very difficult for him to exert any power against you should he manage to get his arms between your body and his. Keep your elbows well up into his arm-pits.

(b) Your hips must be kept on the mats, the weight of your body being slumped on your opponent.

(c) Your legs must be well spread out and the toes dug into the mats. Your hips and feet make the three legs of a tripod and naturally, the wider you spread the legs of a tripod the more secure it becomes.

(*d*) At all times in this hold you must keep your body in a straight line with that of your opponent—the further you allow yourself to be forced away from his position, the weaker will your hold become.

Variations to the Upper Four Quarter Hold

It is not always easy or even possible to place yourself in the correct basic position for the Upper Four Quarter Hold against strenuous resistance from your opponent. If unable to obtain the usual grip, you will find it almost as

Fig. 36

effective—many Black Belts consider it better—to place one or both your arms outside your opponent's arms (Fig. 36).

Another popular variation is to bring your knees up to your opponent's shoulders, dropping your hips towards the mats (Fig. 37). When adopting this method it is difficult to keep relaxed and this weakness should be watched, especially as it is often necessary to drop one leg

Fig. 37

back to maintain your hold. This hold is impossible to maintain if the body is tensed.

Method of Escape from Holds—General Principles

It must be remembered that a hold once correctly

applied cannot be broken unless the person applying the hold makes a mistake. Counters to these holds therefore fall into two classes, that of avoiding falling victim to a hold and secondly finding means of persuading your opponent into an error once you have become his victim on the ground. Groundwork usually follows an attempted throw which although it brings one or both contestants to the mats is not sufficiently clean to obtain a point. If you have been brought down in this manner and your opponent has remained standing and retained his hold on your right sleeve, he is in an ideal position to follow you down into a hold down—usually the Scarf Hold (page 40). If then you are brought down but a point is not awarded, you must immediately take action to avoid being held. Your action must be more than immediate if this is possible, it must be so instinctive that you do not even take the time required to think of it. Once on the ground you must curl up your body—this should have been done to take the fall—and roll over to face your opponent at the same time bringing up your right leg, if your opponent is at your right side, so that your knee is against your elbow. This prevents your opponent bringing his leg close against your body, a necessary step to control on the

ground (Fig. 38). From this position it is not difficult to revolve your body so that your legs are towards your opponent and then drive him away to enable you to spring up. It is possible to throw from this position with your legs and the method of doing this is described later, as is the correct method of regaining your feet without leaving yourself open to attack whilst doing so.

Fig. 38

Breaking a hold once it is applied against you presents

far greater difficulties. Once your opponent has obtained contact with your body he can sense and anticipate your movements to a great extent depending on his experience and ability. Your only hope is to bluff or force him into an error and this is often not as difficult as it appears. It is a strange fact that exponents of judo are divided into two groups, those who like and are good at groundwork and those who do very little and are really bad. Even high grade judoka tend to fall into these categories. Seldom do you find anyone who could be described as average. Similarly groundwork ability is seldom related to the ability of the judoka with the standing up side of the sport such as the throws. Despite this, groundwork practice carried out correctly, will improve your throws and general movements standing up from the earliest stages of your judo career.

Should you fail to deny your opponent his hold, you must immediately attempt to break the hold before he has it firmly secured. In other words, do not let him settle down as once he has done this the problem is greatly magnified. When a hold down is applied, there are obviously two people concerned; one of these—yourself—being held wishes to change the positions, the other, your opponent, does not. Now it is obviously far more easy to move the body which desires to move, your own, than the body which does not, your opponent, and who will resist strongly. In other words always attempt to move your own body and not that of your opponent. This is the first basic principle of groundwork. The second basic principle is always attempt to control your opponent's hips because as you move your body he will try to follow but this can be prevented if you have this control and thus prevent his free movement. The usual method of obtaining this control is to grip your opponent's belt.

Method of Escape from Upper Four Quarter Hold

The first essential is to form a gap between your body

and that of your opponent. In order to do this, bridge
or arch your body (Fig. 51 on page 90) and push your
opponent away from you with a grip on his belt or clothing at his hips. As you come down, keep your arms straight
as possible and push your body away from that of your
opponent with your arms so that he is now at arms length.
Immediately bridge again and, maintaining contact, turn
your body to your left—the right of course is equally
effective—bringing your left hip and leg under your right

Fig. 39

and pressing your left foot hard on the mat as soon as the
movement is completed (Fig. 39). Now continue to turn
your body to your left by bringing your right hip over
your left and turning until you have turned completely

Fig. 40

over with both feet firmly on the mat (Fig. 40). If you
maintain contact with your opponent, he will be turned
with you and rolled over, the positions being reversed.

Methods of Escape from the Scarf Hold Down

Your opponent has obtained this hold on you and is
sitting at your right side. The key to the position is his

control of your right arm; if you can break that control, you should be able to free your hips and escape or even reverse the positions. Therefore your initial efforts must be devoted to freeing your right arm from his grip. If you just pull your arm away, you will develop little power and will fail in your effort. What you must do is take your right shoulder and hip away from his hold in one movement, thus using the combined power of the whole of your body. If you choose an opportune moment for this move you should free your arm sufficiently to form a small gap between you and be able to get your arm under his body and use it as a powerful lever. You can often bluff your opponent into giving you the opportunity for this move by first pushing him and then, as he pushes back at you—of course he should not do this but it is a natural reaction—release your arm just as described. The main object is to obtain space between you and the person holding you down. Once this is done, all your main difficulties are overcome.

Your right elbow being safely under his body and a grip on his belt being affected with your free left hand (Fig. 41), you can, by withdrawing your right hip, make a space between yourself and your opponent. Now you can either bring up your right knee into the gap and against his body and roll him over your own

Fig. 41

body to your left where you can apply a hold down of your own, or you can continue to withdraw your hip and body until you are completely clear of him.

It is often possible to make a gap between you and your

opponent by withdrawing your right hip and then hooking your left leg round his left thigh. Again from here you can roll him over your body so that he falls at your left side. By the rules of judo a hold of this type is automatically deemed to be broken if you can hook and hold your opponent's leg above the knee with your own leg.

To avoid discouragement it must be pointed out that if at first these methods are not very effective, it is probably because the hold is correctly applied and once any hold is correctly applied and maintained against you it cannot be broken. You can only hope to persuade your opponent into making an error and then seize your opportunity. This requires a great deal of experience in timing and anticipation of your opponent's movements.

"Figure 4" Arm Lock from the Scarf Hold Down

This is an arm lock which is most effective against an opponent who attempts to break your hold down by pushing you away from him with his arms by sheer strength. This is a mistake very often made by beginners and even fairly experienced men.

You have obtained the Scarf Hold on your opponent, against his right side, and he with his right hand attempts to break your hold by pushing against your face or jaw. Immediately grasp his wrist with your left hand and push his hand and wrist under your right thigh (Fig. 42), his arm

Fig. 42

being bent as in the "Figure 4" Arm Lock already described on page 49. Hold his hand and wrist against the mats with your right thigh and apply the pressure by raising your right hip. It should be remembered that as it is not easy to judge the amount of pressure being applied against your opponent's arm when using your leg to obtain a lock, care should be taken not to cause damage through too great enthusiasm. Often you will find that if you follow your opponent's movement as you must for success the pressure of his arm is more downward towards your hip and not upward against your pull. In this case take his right arm down and lock it under your left thigh and apply the lock by raising that thigh.

Occasionally you will find that a strong opponent will manage to straighten his arm to prevent it being locked under your thigh. In these circumstances, assist him to straighten his arm and

Fig. 43

this time push his hand and wrist under the calf of your right leg (Fig. 43). Once more hold his wrist against the mats with your leg, applying the lock by raising your right hip. Again this lock must be applied slowly and with care.

CHAPTER VIII

LESSON 7

The Standing Neck Lock

This is another type of Neck Lock, but is again one of those applied against the carotid arteries. This lock has the advantage that it can be applied against an opponent who is standing, especially if he is crouched forward or is looking down watching your feet. As you will have realised, most neck and strangle holds are only effective on the ground as it is otherwise very difficult to obtain the required leverage even if you can find the opening which is most unlikely.

The opportunity arises when your opponent, probably in an effort to avoid your throws, crouches and leans forward. This is a habit which can easily develop from lack of an active instructor and therefore requires particular attention from readers. To avoid giving warning, slip your right hand from his lapel and on to his collar fairly deep and beneath but slightly to the rear of his ear. This move does not as a rule present much difficulty.

The movement of the left hand from his sleeve is not as easy because your object is clear and the move must be made rapidly to avoid giving undue warning. It must be placed in a similar position taking a grip on the left of his collar

Fig. 44

(your opponent's right). (See Fig. 44).

The palms of your hands should be upper most so that your knuckles are against his neck below and a little behind his ears. Obtain firm contact by turning your wrists upwards—so that the palms of your hands are turned more directly upwards—and then slide your hands forward, towards you, as in the Normal Cross Strangle Hold (page 61) and for the same reason, that of displacing the muscles protecting this carotid arteries. Now increase the pressure

Fig. 45.

by turning your wrists a little more so that your fists revolve on the collar of your opponent's jacket and your knuckles drive more deeply into his neck, at the same time pull his neck down towards your chest stepping back if necessary (Fig. 45). Release the hold as soon as your opponent signals his submission. You will find it more easy to apply the lock if you take a step or two backwards taking your opponent with you.

Essential Points in the Standing Neck Lock

There are one or two essential points which should be emphasised if you are to make this lock act instantaneously as it must to be really effective. It can be a deadly lock and well worth practising if only because an attempt to use it on a defensive, crouching opponent will usually frighten him into straightening up and leave him more open to other forms of attack even if the lock itself fails. First study the position of the hands. It is the wrist movement which obtains contact and applies the pressure for the lock. It is essential that the person applying the lock pulls his opponent's head down on to his own chest because this weakens his position and makes it almost impossible for him to resist. Should he be very strong and still manage somehow to resist take a step backwards taking him with you.

Note

It will help if you keep your elbows fairly close together as this tends to prevent your opponent placing his arms between your elbows and levering them apart to avoid the lock.

The Forward Rolling Breakfall

You will all have heard and most of you will have seen films or pictures of the famous Stomach Throw—the throw with which the smallest judo expert can send much larger and stronger opponents hurtling over their heads. Although many of the stories told of this throw are pure fables and others much exaggerated, you can rest assured that this throw is powerful in effect and against certain types of resistance amazingly easy to perform. However, it is better to leave all that until later when you have learnt how to breakfall to the throw. Until you are able to perform a good breakfall of the type required, the throw is far too severe to attempt in case it is tried on you in turn.

First study Fig. 46. Notice how the Black Belt demon-

strating the breakfall has his right leg forward and is ready to place his right hand on the mats in front of his right foot. His head is well tucked in preparatory to making a smooth roll forward his wrist is turned to avoid a sprain or similar injury.

Fig. 46

Now he rolls forward keeping his right arm straight beneath him as he does so (Fig. 47). This straight arm prevents his head striking the mats as he goes over. He continues to roll until he finishes in a normal breakfall position beating the mats hard with his left arm.

Examine Fig. 47 more carefully noticing that the roll is being made over the right shoulder. The body revolves in a complete half-circle over the right arm and then the right shoulder being in a continuous curve thus allows you to make a smooth roll and finish with the breakfall you have already practiced.

The fact that the right arm is kept straight is very important. If you allow the arm to collapse, your circular movement will be broken and you will stand a first class chance of landing on your head—with painful

Fig. 47

results. Do not make the arm completely rigid as this endangers the elbow in the case of your making a bad fall. The arm should be kept straight and pass beneath you as you roll forward over it—Figs. 47 and 48 show this clearly.

A common fault is to place both hands on the mats and perform a kind of tumbler's roll. This inevitably results in an extremely unpleasant jar to the spine and could cause serious injury. The left hand must not touch the mats until you beat with it in your breakfall. Until you are able to conquer this

Fig. 48

tendency to place the left hand on the mats in order to assist your roll you will not succeed in making a successful breakfall of this type. Wrestlers have a tendency to bridge their body to avoid being thrown on their shoulders. In theory this does avoid losing a point as they are not thrown cleanly on to the mat but it is a very dangerous method, having a good chance of causing an injury to the neck or back. Also, an experienced opponent can overcome this method of avoiding the throw but this results in a very severe and possibly dangerous fall. Under no circumstances should the reader adopt this method of avoiding the stomach throw even though in the early stages it may prove successful.

As progress is made, the breakfall can be further developed. As you must have noticed, a ball dropped straight down on to the ground will bounce whilst if it is thrown forward it will land smoothly and roll along. To take this illustration still further, imagine a brick instead of a ball. in this case a brick dropped straight on to the ground will chip or break up completely but if it is thrown forward it will roll or slide along the ground receiving little or no damage. This is the theory on which this fall is based, for it is obvious that the judo exponent does not wish to be broken up like the brick; it is far more comfortable to roll into a smooth breakfall when we take a Stomach Throw. You have been told this before in Lesson 1 but it merits repetition.

For these reasons it is essential to spread out on the fall. To do this you must reach forward with your right hand as far as you possibly can with comfort and then allow your body to roll over your outstretched arm which is once more kept straight. It is not advisable to attempt this at once but rather to spread out your breakfall gradually until you have the confidence and ability to make the fall with a run reaching forward as far as possible with the right hand.

If you are left-handed or prefer to roll over your left arm breaking your fall with your right by all means do so. In fact you must learn to make this and all falls and of course the throws, holds and locks on either side with equal skill as the side on which you breakfall may well depend on which foot your opponent uses for his throw.

The Side Four Quarters Hold Down ("T" Hold Down)

This is another most effective method of holding an opponent helpless with practically no effort on your own part. Basically it is very similar to the Upper Four Quarter Hold already described on page 73. It is sometimes called the "T" hold for reasons that will be quite obvious if you look at the position of the judoka in Fig. 49. Examine the diagram more thoroughly imagining that you are looking down on the hold as it is being demonstrated. The person being held is lying on his back on the mats and you lie across him as shown in Fig. 49. Lie so that your chest is on his body, your head over his left side and your

Fig. 49

legs extended to his right. Your left arm slips under his head and takes a grip deep on his jacket underneath him somewhere in the vicinity of his left shoulderblade. This prevents him turning in towards you. Your right arm is thrust in between his legs and grips his belt in the middle of his back. If you hold to one side he may be able to brace his thigh against your right arm and by straightening his body, apply too much strength against your arm for you to hold and break your grip on his belt, and, even worse, you may find your arm pinned between his legs when, as may happen, the hold is broken.

As in the Upper Four Quarter Hold Down, the weight of your chest is dropped on to his body and greatly assists in exhausting him, even before he makes any violent movement, by restricting his breathing. Your hips are dropped on to the mats close to your opponent's right side, whilst your legs are thrust out straight behind you. Have your legs spread out as far as possible with your toes dug well into the mats.

Providing you take up this position, there are many variations, and if your body is relaxed you should have no difficulty when your opponent struggles in an attempt to release himself. If he attempts to turn to his right, lifting the left side of his body, drop the weight of your chest down on him pushing forward from your toes—on **no account** lift your hips from the mats. If you push forward from your knees instead of your toes you will find it impossible to prevent your hips lifting from the mats and you should be thrown right over him to land on your back at his left side.

If your opponent tries to force you down towards his feet, attempting to sit up, hold him down with the weight of your chest forcing him back by using the pressure of the toes of your right foot on the mats. Your legs should be well spread out, thus giving you the maximum amount of leverage against the mats (Fig. 49). Should he make an attempt to arch or bridge his body and so throw you over his head, pressure on your right toes will counteract his effort.

When you are finally satisfied with this hold, you should attempt it from the left, transferring all the instructions to the opposite side.

A Variation of the Side Four Quarter Hold

A popular variation which is taught in many clubs is

shown in Fig. 50. When this method is adopted, the knees are drawn up close to your opponent's body and assist in preventing his efforts to turn or roll out of your hold. At first glance this method appears to

Fig. 50

break one of the basic rules of groundwork—keep the hips on the mat—but actually this is not so. The hips must be lowered firmly down towards the mats but do not force them down as this will prevent relaxation. Your knees are placed firmly against his body to prevent him getting his arm beneath your body and using them as levers to throw you off.

Should your opponent's efforts to escape become dangerous, you can usually regain control by throwing back your right or left leg as necessary according to the direction of his movements. You can even drop back to the original form of the hold (Fig. 49).

Personally, I do not like this variation as I find it difficult to retain control and usually finish up applying the original method in order to retain my hold. I also find the variation more easy to break but I know several Black Belts who can apply it most successfully and have done so with me as the victim on many occasions.

Groundwork—General Principles—Breaking Holds

There is a general tendency to make groundwork a battle of strength. Strong, heavy judoka find that their weight results in their opponent being unable to break their holds and so they get the undeserved reputation of groundwork "experts." A groundwork contest of this type is very ugly and uninteresting to watch and in grading contests will seriously delay promotion. Alternatively, good groundwork is enjoyable to watch, requires no undue strength and is a great advantage in contests because your opponent knowing your ability on the ground fears to attack as a failure will probably result in groundwork.

Successful groundwork just as much as successful throws depends on the application of a good judo technique. The following movements as well as being used to break holds are also very helpful judo exercises, being equally useful for both throws and groundwork for the reason that the basic technique for both ground and standing work is exactly the same.

As explained in a previous lesson it is essential in order to break a hold that your efforts are aimed at moving your own body and not that of your opponent. To do this you must, if only for a fraction of a second, form a gap or space between your body and his. The usual and probably the best method is to bridge your body either like a

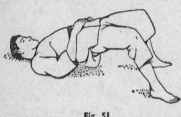

wrestler from the head or, as is more usual in judo, as we do not develop the powerful neck of a wrestler, from the shoulders (Fig. 51). Bridge with the soles of the feet flat on the

Fig. 51

mat thus raising your whole body from feet to shoulders. It is obvious that at this stage you can lower your body to the mat at will and as you, and not your opponent, select the time to do this you can, as you come down, obtain the required gap between you. To increase this your arms should be straightened as you come down— you have already been taught to hold your opponent's

Fig. 52

belt in order to control his hips as soon as you are held—
and in the case of a Scarf Hold (page 79) withdraw your
right hip keeping the arms straight as you do so. This either
enables you to bring up your right knee or forces your
opponent to attempt to close the gap, which enables you
to roll him over your body as he makes his effort to do so.

In the case of the Side or Upper Four Quarter Holds
the principle is the same, the body is bridged and the arms,
holding his belt to control the hips, are straightened.
Straighten the arms by withdrawing your body, not
pushing your opponent away (Fig. 52). Again the hip is
withdrawn, your body being revolved in the gap formed
by use of the hips, the hip being withdrawn always
passing beneath the other. Note how the foot on the

mat is pressed
firmly into it,
enabling you to
use the whole
power of the
body in the
movement (Fig.
53). It is essen-
tial to utilise
your full power
both standing
and on the
ground as you
are certain at
some time,
whatever your
strength, to meet

Fig. 53

a stronger opponent. This need not matter as it is the
operative strength which has effect. If, for example, the
sum of your strength is 10 units and that of your opponent,
who may be taken as being twice as strong, is 20, you
do not appear to have much chance. But if through the use

of sound technique that you are able to utilise 9 of your units against an opponent who only utilises a quarter of his strength, say 5 units, you are in the position of being able to apply superior power at any given time. Believe me this is no mere example but common experience in judo contests. Adapt these movements, without an opponent, as a series of exercises.

Groundwork — General Principles — Retaining Holds Against Opposition

Breaking holds is not easy but can be done if correct technique is applied. Equally important is to retain your own hold once the opportunity arises and the hold is secured. Once more if you meet strength with strength you will always fall to superior power. This can be avoided if you observe three rules.

1. Keep your body completely relaxed.
2. Keep your hips on the mats.
3. Keep the same relative position between your own body and that of your opponent.

The first needs very little explaining but only if you are relaxed can you observe the second and third rules. Also complete relaxation allows you to foil your opponent's movements in their early stages and take appropriate action.

The second rule has been mentioned in the individual holds described. This is necessary to prevent your opponent's efforts to obtain a lever against you by placing his knee or arm beneath your body.

Rule three again needs no explaining for once you have allowed your opponent to move without any corresponding movement from you, he will be able to obtain such a position that your hold is no longer applied against his body.

A fourth rule might well have been added. This is "Never attempt to retain a hold once your opponent has begun to escape." Once your hold has commenced to slip, your opponent will find no difficulty in making his escape and will usually succeed in rolling you over and applying a hold on you.

As your hold slips, allow your body to move in the direction to which your opponent is applying his counter attack. If your hold is the Scarf Hold (Fig. 16 on page 40) and your opponent manages to free his right arm and shoulder, you might, for example, scissor your legs— your right hip being pulled back under your left—never the left moved over the right as this would lift your hips from the mats—and roll your body so that your chest is

Fig. ·54

pressed down on his chest, keeping your hips down on the mat (Fig. 54). As the opportunity arises you can now move back to your Scarf Hold or change it to a Side Four Quarter Hold.

Similarly from a Side Four Quarter you can release your right hand and place it on his belt at your opponent's right side. Keeping the hips on the mat it is easy to slide round into an Upper Four Quarters transferring your left hand when the opportunity occurs. From here you can transfer to a Side Four Quarters or Scarf Hold on your opponent's left if you wish to do so.

As an alternative it is possible from say a Scarf Hold against your opponent's right to scissor your legs as already described and then to bring your right leg, controlled by your hip (Fig. 55) across your opponent's body, thus transferring your form of attack. The movement must be made from the hip, the leg following and being

kept against his body the whole time. If you fail to do this, he will prevent your movement with his right leg.

This is actually quite advanced judo and well ahead of the stage you

Fig 55

have reached but the movements are so useful and the exercise so valuable to both throws and groundwork that I have included them at this point. I suggest also that you refer back to these General Principles whenever you are learning groundwork.

Methods of Escape from the Side Four Quarters Hold ("T" Hold)

It must be pointed out once more that if you are trapped by this or any hold correctly applied you will be unable to escape unless your opponent makes an error. Therefore no efforts will be made to show you any standard "tricks" for escape but will rather give you some hints on how to force your opponent into a mistake and then take advantage of his lapse.

When you lie on your back on the mats there are five possible directions in which you can move. They are to your left and right, towards your feet and head and finally upwards by bridging your body. To go downwards is, of course, impossible. Therefore these are the basic directions against which anyone attempting a hold must be prepared to move in counter-action against his opponent's attempt to escape.

If, when you are being held down, you move towards your feet, attempting to sit up for example, the counter will be for the "holder" to force you back by downward pressure of his chest, the power coming from the action of the toes of his right foot against the mats. Immediately the holder presses towards your head, bridge your body, this will give you room to insert your right arm under him and grip the front of his belt, bringing your left arm over his body and clasp the back of his belt with your hand. This leaves you in a very strong defensive position but the the final method of escape depends on your opponent's reactions. He will probably do one of two things; he may push forward to prevent you escaping to your left, in which case assist him to go in that direction by lifting and pulling to your left with your hands, at the same time turning your hips and body hard to your left and, should the move be made smoothly and correctly timed, your opponent will turn a complete circle and fall on his back at your left side. Take care not to damage his neck.

Alternatively should your opponent anticipate or feel your intention to move to your left and attempt to hold you back by slipping his hips back a little and thus prevent your right hip being raised off the mats, you must take action in a different direction. This time push him to your right with both hands on his belt in the positions already described and slide your body away from underneath him. You should find yourself completely free.

There are several other methods but they all depend on obtaining the control of his hips which has been described. This control of his hips means control of the movement of the whole of his body. The other methods can be discovered for yourself by experience and practice and are all based on those already shown.

The Stomach Throw

On no account should you attempt to learn this spectacular and most effective throw until you are fully satisfied that you are proficient in carrying out the breakfall described in Lesson 7 on page 84. Also in the interests of safety it is necessary to ensure that your opponent has been taught the breakfall. It is essential that, if either of you are not satisfied with your breakfall, you practise until it is effective. Never take any risks with this violent throw.

If you use the normal hold on your opponent's jacket, the opportunity for this throw arises when your opponent is keeping his feet well away from you by leaning forward. You are certain to have noticed by now that some people, especially the strong type, develop the habit of avoiding Ankle and similar throws by holding you well away with their arms in order that you cannot reach their feet. The position thus adopted is hopeless from their point of view because not only are they unable to attack you but they also leave themselves open to many throws far more violent than the Ankle Throws which they seek to avoid. Of these the Stomach Throw is one of the most severe and effective but is by no means the only one.

The ideal position in which to have your opponent for the throw is leaning towards you with his body curved slightly forward. Similarly your body should be slightly curved. Remember that throughout the throw it should be possible to imagine a circle can be drawn between both of your bodies, and this has to be retained throughout the throw.

When your opponent takes up this position draw him

forward with your hands at the same time gliding your left foot in between his feet. Notice how the circle is maintained once more like a huge ball between your own body and that of your opponent. Continue the pull and sit down smoothly as near as possible to your own left heel (Fig 56) simultaneously bringing your right foot

Fig. 56

gently up into your opponent's abdomen just below his belt. Now in exactly the same way that you practiced in the preliminary stage of the backward breakfall in Lesson 1 on page 22 roll backwards and you will find that your opponent will roll over your right foot and fall to the mats on his back behind you (Fig 57).

Fig. 57

That is all there is to the throw in general which is amazingly simple in theory but not in practice. To bring it off successfully, it is necessary to break it up into sections in order to study the basic movements in more detail.

Essential Points in the Stomach Throw

(*a*) As in all throws it is essential to break your opponent's balance. There are two ways in which this may be done. In both you must curve your body forward but there are two methods by which you can make use of the power given you by this position. Opinions differ greatly on this point but it must depend on your own build and on that of your opponent. You can turn your wrists downward and press down from the wrist action as you curve your body. This method is better if your opponent is shorter than yourself or you can lift by turning your wrists upwards. This method is generally used against an opponent who is taller than yourself. In any case, whichever method you finally favour, do not decide definitely until you have practised each for a considerable time and always remember that the curve of the body and the movements which follow are the most vital points in the throw. It is amazing how many holders of high grades who have been practising judo for years suddenly decide that the other method is better than their own and change over to it. Never be afraid to try any new method that may be shown to you.

(*b*) Continue to break your opponent's balance with your wrists and by curving your body at the same time gliding your left foot forward along the mats between his feet as far as possible whilst **retaining** your own balance, and bending your right knee.

(*c*) Still retaining the curve of your body sit down on your own left heel, or as near to it as you possible can, then just roll backwards keeping your head tucked in to prevent it breaking your circular roll back. Your opponent will wheel over you just as if you were the hub of a wheel and he was the outer rim. Watch that his head does not strike your face. As you do this, bring the sole of your right foot up into his abdomen making only gentle contact, and use this foot to help guide him over.

On no account thrust him upwards as to do so will spoil the rhythm and circular movement of your throw. This will not only cause it to fail but may bring him down on top of you, which can be most unpleasant to both you and your opponent.

(*d*) When practising this throw with a friend, perform it slowly, especially at first. This will give you time to learn the correct movement whilst you "victim" will be able to practise and improve his breakfall. Your mistakes will be more obvious when you attempt this, or any other throw, slowly and you will greatly benefit by using this method from time to time with all movements.

CHAPTER IX

LESSON 8

How to Defend Yourself when Brought Down and How to Get Up from the Mats

As in all sports the umpire's decision is final but judo leaves even more to his personal opinion than most other sports. For this reason you must stop immediately you are told to do so by the umpire's call of "stop" and should continue at all other times until "Point" or "Time" is called. The umpire will always stop the contest if he considers it necessary to do so in the interests of safety.

By now you will have found that, whilst you manage to get your opponent to the mats fairly often, only a small proportion of these efforts are sufficiently clean to merit the award of a point. If then you are brought down you are, with your opponent standing over you, at a great disadvantage. He is in a good position to follow you down for a hold, especially if he has retained control of your inside arm (that is your right arm if you are thrown to your right). Your first move must be to break away by pulling your arm free (for this description I shall assume a right hand throw which means your opponent is standing at your right side), and bring up your right leg so that your right knee and elbow meet (Fig. 38, page 76). Now you must turn immediately so that you face him, thus enabling you to use your legs in defence Never kick out at your opponent at this stage as not only from the sport point of view is it dangerous but it is also ineffective. It is easy to ward off your leg as it straightens and then you have no further defence to offer. With correct movement you have a very good chance to get up but in order

Fig. 58

to do so keep facing your opponent using your legs as a threat. As opportunity arises bring your right leg back and place on the mats as far back as possible (Fig. 58). Now push up on your right arm and spring up away from your opponent. As you do so use your left arm to protect your head from attack.

A Leg Throw from the Ground

There is an alternative to getting to your feet when, as it is termed in judo, "half-thrown." Force your opponent away from you as just described turning to face him whilst still on the ground. Instead of bringing your right foot back to spring to your feet, catch your opponent's leg, the one nearest to you, with your right foot just behind his ankle (Fig 59) as you do so bringing the sole of your left foot up and pushing firmly against the same leg

Fig. 59

just below the knee. Unless he turns very quickly to release his leg, he will be thrown cleanly on to his back and even should he succeed in avoiding your attack, he will be a fair distance from you and you can get to your feet at your leisure.

Judo Throws—General Principles—3

So far, whilst practising your throws, you have been taught to retain a grip on your opponent's jacket with your left hand. That is the side on which he does not require to breakfall—the inside of the circle. This has been done in order that you may assist him to make a correct breakfall but it was also pointed out that there were other important reasons why this should be done. How important this action really is in judo will now be explained.

You have just been told what happens when your opponent fails to obtain a clean effective throw as a result of his efforts. In a real fight your opponent would not be disabled if you brought him down in this way and in a judo contest you would not obtain a point for a clean throw unless he is thrown cleanly on his back. However there are means of concluding the fight or contest rapidly and successfully in your favour from this position and they are fairly easy to learn only depending on this retention of your hold on your opponent's jacket. This leaves you an opening to apply a hold down or an arm lock but take care to avoid the leg throw just described.

The Straight Arm Lock from a Throw

For the purpose of teaching this hold I will assume you have thrown your opponent with a Drawing Ankle Throw to your left retaining a grip on his right sleeve with your left hand and checking his fall correctly (see Fig. 38 on page 76). This time, instead of stepping away after having checked him and allowing him to rise to his feet to continue practice, retain the hold on his sleeve as he falls. Keep his arm straight and maintain sufficient tension to lift his right side slightly thus preventing him adopting a defensive position against you. Still retaining the tension on your opponent's arm to keep it straight, glide your left foot round his head and sit down on, or as near to as possible, your own right heel. If the movement with which you made the throw is correct your right foot will be close to the side of his body without further movement but if necessary move your foot so that it is this position and, keeping his arm straight, roll back bringing his arm between your thighs and using your thighs to grip the arm firmly (Figs. 17 and 18 on pages 44 and 45) as described on page 44 which deals with the theory of this hold.

It is essential that the tension on your opponent's arm be maintained throughout and that you apply the lock by sitting down on your right heel before you finally pull the arm back between your thighs. If you fail to do this and instead fall back, there is a serious danger of an injury to your opponent's arm and, even if you avoid this, you will usually fail to obtain a submission once you are down.

The remainder of the lock is applied exactly as described in Lesson 2 on page 44 which deals with the Straight Arm Lock.

If you have a friend available you should practice these movements conscientiously, very slowly and carefully, turning back to Lesson 2 for further details as required, you then begin to speed up, commencing to apply the lock almost before your opponent has hit the mats from your throw. Although you have been told to fall back at an angle greater than 90 degrees to your opponent's body (not in the form of a letter "T") in order that you can pull his arm down over your thigh you will find that you will be able to modify this lock and still apply it effectively.

Often you may find yourself at an angle of considerably less than 90 degrees to your opponent's body, but even here it is possible to apply the lock from these alternative positions. However, concentrate on the correct basic movements and positions and allow these variations to develop with experience.

Remember that if at any time in practice or in contest you find yourself in danger of losing your balance whilst applying this lock you must let go immediately otherwise an injury may result.

The Scarf Hold from a Throw

In judo, particularly in team contests, you will often find that your opponent will not let go of you even when you are obviously in a position to throw him. As a result you usually allow him to escape for the sake of safety. Actually experienced judo exponents, especially in contests, overcome this difficulty by completing the throw and if it is not quite sufficiently clean to obtain a point they still find themselves in position for a hold down and secure the point that way.

This is a good opportunity to point out that when an experienced judo exponent forces his throw against an opponent who hangs on to him that opponent is usually shaken by the violence of the fall. This method of forcing a point should never be used by a comparative beginner and even high grades must take great care and ensure that they take precautions.

Providing that you are now able to make a clean throw and also apply a Scarf Hold direct from the throw without undue chance of causing damage to your opponent, this very useful combination of throw and hold may be practised.

From the normal hold you throw your opponent with a Hip Throw checking him correctly as he falls. Once more retain the tension on his right arm and this time drop your body at his right side as he hits the mats, pulling his right arm to your left and holding it between your left arm, left thigh and abdomen. On no account fall on his body, drop at his side so that your right hip falls on the mats—as close to his side as possible—without actually falling directly on him—and slip your right arm round his neck finishing up in the Scarf Hold position already shown in Fig. 16 on page 40.

Be prepared to take the weight of your body on your right hand should you find yourself in danger of falling with your weight on your opponent's body. It is just as easy to place your hand on the mats as it is to slide your arm round his neck.

This only shows you how to adopt this hold down from a clean throw from the normal standing position. Actually in a contest there would be no object in continuing on the ground after a throw as a point would be awarded and the contestants ordered to their feet. The chief use of this method occurs when your throw is not quite good enough and your opponent only stumbles and drops to one knee or his side. At this stage, you are able to obtain your hold by pulling his right arm to your left, round your body, and placing your right arm round his neck or body. Continue turning to your left, as you do so. Finally, if you drop your right hip to the ground you can use the weight of your body to drive him to the mats in a regulation hold down.

There is another very common use for this hold. Frequently when you come into position for a Hip or Shoulder Throw your opponent will, even if he is lifted clean off his feet, hang on to your back however good your movement or position may have been. Should this occur, you will find it impossible to make your throw by the methods so far shown. From this Hip Throw position with your opponent "hanging on" to you use your left arm to pull his right arm hard round you and continue to turn to your left, all the time holding him close to your body with your right arm round his waist, and throw yourself in that direction (to your left) so that you fall to the mats with your opponent beneath you. As you fall, remove your right arm from its position round his body in order that his weight does not damage your arm and immediately slide it round his neck for the hold down. You should make sure that the weight of your body is taken on your right hip on the mat as you fall so that you do not damage your opponent by crushing his ribs with the weight of your body. However careful you are, your opponent will be severely shaken and after a few similar experiences will soon stop the dangerous, annoying and ineffective habit of hanging on to you to avoid being thrown.

The Leg Wheel Throw

This is another popular and extremely useful throw. Similar in many ways to the Body Drop, it is ideal for the tall man or anyone practising with an opponent shorter than himself but should by no means be restricted to such circumstances. It is normally effective against anyone who is tending to lean forward with straight legs, but variations can make it effective to the side or rear although in the latter case it is really a different throw—the Major Outer Reaping.

It is better to deal with the basic throw and allow you to discover the variations from your own experience. This basic throw, as already stated, is carried out to the front of an opponent who tends to lean forward with straight legs, probably to avoid an Ankle Throw. The foot movement is exactly the same as shown for the Body Drop which was illustrated in Fig. 22 on page 52. Step back and pass your left foot behind your own right foot, as you do so taking your left hip back, keeping it over the foot all the time, and drawing your opponent with your arms in a circular movement in exactly the same direction. When your left foot has been placed on the mat to the left (your opponent's left)

Fig. 60

and slightly in front of his left foot, bring your right hip through between you, placing the back of your straight right leg just above the heel across the front of his right leg at slightly below knee level (Fig. 60). Draw back your left hip continuing your movement to the left and bringing your own left elbow down towards your left knee (Fig. 60). Your opponent, being unable to step forward to regain his balance because of your right leg, will be wheeled over your leg and fall to the mats in front of you. Maintain firm pressure against him with your right leg throughout the final phase of the throw.

Essential Points in the Leg Wheel Throw

(*a*) Bring your left foot behind your right and place it as far to your left as you can, beside your opponent's left foot if possible—your own left foot turned so that your toes point as far as you can get them to your left, that is to say in the direction of your throw. As you move your foot back, bring your hip round with it, thus keeping your balance over the foot all the time. Lower your left hip by bending your knee as you turn.

(*b*) As you move your left hip and foot back and round, curve your body slightly forward (Fig. 60) and bring your left elbow down towards your well bent left knee. Similarly, as you turn you must bring your opponent round with you in order to break his balance, i.e. draw him round to your left in a circular movement with your hands.

(*c*) As soon as you are securely balanced on your left foot, bring your right leg through and place it against the front of your opponent's right leg just below his knee. Your leg should be kept straight with the toes pointed. Firm pressure must be maintained against your opponent's leg by the use of your hip but on no account must you attempt to kick or hook your opponent's legs away. This is a common and dangerous habit with some beginners and does not add to the effectiveness of the throw actually lessening it because of the jerky movement.

(*d*) Maintaining the pressure against his leg and continuing to turn to your left by withdrawing your left hip, bring your elbow down towards your left knee and simultaneously drive your opponent's body round by the pull and push of your left and right arms respectively. As a result he should be wheeled over your outstretched right leg to the mats.

The theory of this throw is that you upset your opponent's balance and at just the time he would normally slip forward to recover you place your right leg in his way. This removes his last means of recovery and he therefore falls to the mats in front of you. Your turning movement to your left takes your own body out of the line of his movement.

CHAPTER X

LESSON 9

Judo Throws—General Principles—4

In all throws it is essential to exert the pull or push of your arms in exactly the direction of your own body movement. This has been mentioned several times but it is so vital that emphasis is essential. For example, take the normal hold on your opponent and by withdrawing your left hip turn to your left at the same time drawing your opponent round you with your left hand without any individual movement of hand or arm Thus your hand, arm, shoulder and hip work is in conjunction with your body, operating as one complete unit, the hip being the axis. This movement is reasonably straightforward and fairly simple to perform, the difficulty in practice arises with the right arm and leading opinions vary considerably regarding the actual movement. This main principle is however generally accepted—the push of the right arm must follow exactly the line taken by the left arm just as the left arm must follow the line taken by the left hip and foot.

The pivot is made on the right hip which must not be advanced but should act as the point of a geometrical compass around which the left hip is revolved. It is essential that the right hand and arm do not describe a wider arc than the left. If this occurs, you will find that you have pushed your opponent too far away from you and have given him back his balance and maybe destroyed your own.

Self Defence—General Principles

Since the introduction of unarmed combat into the forces it has been possible to pick up almost any magazine and find one or more advertisements for judo, jujitsu or judo courses usually by correspondence. Unfortunately some of these courses are written and illustrated by people without any judo training, with the result that vital points such as balance and direction of movement are completely ignored making the course valueless. It is for the reason that self-defence is based on instinctive re-action and an automatically correct movement that recognised clubs do not teach it until the member is familiar with the general movements of judo and has obtained a certain amount of control over his body. Then, and not until then, is he taught self-defence. As a general rule the self-defence stage is not reached until the member attains his Black Belt by which time he has realised that judo taught as a sport has produced an instinctive, correct reaction which in emergency would be of far more use than any number of self-defence "tricks" taught by "numbers."

It is only fair to state that these self-defence tricks are in themselves usually quite sound but taught in the "six easy lesson" principle they lose their effectiveness because basic ability, body movement and control from the hips are not there to produce the smoothness and speed so necessary to success. After all, self-defence only consists of meeting any emergency with body and mind in a soft relaxed state in order that immediate response is achieved. If you are mentally tensed considering your opponent's actions and your possible counter to each alternative your success is very unlikely. There are so many variations both to each attacking movement and its natural counter that to learn by the "one, two, three" method is not only wasting time but also gives a totally false impression of your ability which could have serious results if an emergency should arise.

In the following lessons several self-defence throws, locks and holds will be described which when examined in detail will be found to be based on judo movements and obvious variations of those which have already been described.

The Sweeping Loin Throw

There is a really beautiful throw, requiring great skill and control of not only your own balance but also that of your opponent. The name "The Sweeping Loin" is self-explanatory as the throw consists of balancing your opponent on your hip and wheeling him over it to the mats with a sweep or flick of your loins. An extremely graceful throw, it entails sweeping your opponent bodily off the mats in a circular motion whilst balanced on the ball of one foot, and for that reason it leaves the attacker open to counters far more than most of the other throws of the same family such as the various Hip Throws. If, on the other hand, the earlier Lessons have been thoroughly studied and practised, sufficient skill and body control should have been acquired to make it possible for you to learn the Sweeping Loin and perform it successfully.

Fig. 61

This throw may be carried out either to your opponent's side or front according to the direction in which he is moving. As most of the throws described have been against an advancing opponent I shall describe the attack to the side. In this throw your opponent must be brought into an off-balance position to his right front, in other words you must break his balance so that he is forced up on to his toes with his body inclined slightly forward and to his right and with his legs straight. To obtain this position of advantage, face your opponent taking the normal hold on his jacket. Now step to your left, turning your own foot to your left and placing it on the mats to the right and in front of your opponent's right foot (Fig. 61). As you make this step, bend your left knee and also allow your right hand to leave his lapel and place it round his waist under his left arm-pit, sliding it up his back until it comes between his shoulders. Now press his body towards you with a lifting motion of the right hand and arm pulling his chest against your own. Similarly, as you step in with your left foot, use your left arm to pull him to his right also with a slight lift. At this stage, your opponent should have all his weight on his toes, particularly those of his right foot. (See Fig. 62 for this position.)

Now you should find that your right hip is slightly below, outside and to the right of your opponent's right hip. His chest should be in close contact with your body so that he is controlled by your slightest movement and he should be right up on his toes leaning slightly to his right. To complete the throw you bring your right leg through and press it against the outside of your opponent's right thigh and then by flicking

Fig. 62

your right hip backwards as he is pulled on to it your opponent will be swept over your outstretched right leg to the mats.

As an alternative, your right hand can continue to grip the lapel of your opponent's jacket and in this case it must be used to drive him directly to his right (your left), on no account pushing him to his rear. An upward movement must also be used and at the same time the wrist is turned in towards you in order to obtain the body contact described in the previous paragraph.

Essential Points in the Sweeping Loin Throw

(*a*) Step to your left with your left foot placing it outside your opponent's right foot. Turn it to your left as you do so (Fig. 61) bending your knee and curving your body slightly forward.

(*b*) As you step in, use your right arm to obtain contact with your opponent's body and to break his balance to his right by driving him in that direction.

(*c*) Your left hand should lift him to his right and make him move with you as you step in, thus transferring his balance to his right front corner.

(*d*) Bring your right leg and hip through and then, controlling your leg from the hip, thrust it back sweeping his feet from under him. Your leg should be kept straight but not stiff. This sweeping action is made by flicking your right hip back thus sweeping his legs away without any tendency to kick or hack on your part; rather one smooth continuous action.

This is a really beautiful throw when carried out correctly, the whole movement is one unbroken smooth action from the moment you step in with your left foot to your opponent's final breakfall. It is important to remember that you must have close contact with him and he should be lifted only to his toes. If you find that any undue effort is required you should once more work through the theory of the throw to discover the error which you must be making at some point.

Self-Defence—How to Break a Strangle Hold applied from the Front

There are many effective methods of dealing with this

situation but assume for the purpose of practice that your opponent adopts the usual "thug" method of strangling by holding you with both hands, thumbs digging into your throat (Fig. 63). The average person loses his nerve immediately any restriction is placed on his breathing by pressure on the neck or throat and, although this is quite understandable, it plays into the hands of the attacker. This fear of a throat attack is very noticeable in judo with beginners. When one

Fig. 63

first commences judo the first suspicion of a choke or strangle hold obtains a submission but later, as you progress, you become more and more confident and hardened until finally by the time you reach about Green Belt stage you will not submit until you reach the point of unconsciousness. I do not recommend this resistance. It is always better to submit too early than too late.

There should be nothing to fear from a strangle hold or choke lock applied against you when you are standing up. If, as the choke is applied, you simply walk backwards from your attacker, it is impossible for him to maintain any pressure, and should he push forward to make his hold effective, nothing is more simple than to apply a Stomach Throw. Again should the attacker adopt the opposite principle and pull you towards him by the grip on your throat you may find, especially should he be stronger than you, it is impossible to step back, so this time step in and quickly placing one hand, say your left, behind his head, place your right hand beneath his chin

and sharply (very carefully in practice) twist his head to his left (Fig. 64). You will see that an attacker's neck can be broken or severely wrenched with remarkably little effort. This form of counter is therefore forbidden in judo in the interests of safety.

It is better to forget these more violent and crude methods and return to judo. The first means of countering by stepping back and applying a Stomach Throw is sound judo theory, but there is

Fig. 64

another method which is just as effective and avoids the necessity of sacrificing your own upright posture as does a Stomach Throw.

Place your left arm over his right and bring your right arm under his left, clasping your hands together between his arms. Now you will find that by lifting your right arm and forcing down with your left you will upset his balance towards his right front (Fig. 65). If you attain this position not by moving your arms but by lowering and withdrawing your left hip, you will find that your opponent is brought to his toes well off balance to his right and in a perfect position to apply a Body Drop Throw. Continue to turn by withdrawing your left hip and by bending your left

Fig. 65

knee, bringing your right foot through across him as you do so, and placing your ankle against the outside of his right leg as low down as possible as in the Body Drop (Fig. 65). Now, by continuing to turn to your left and bringing your left arm down and raising your right, you will throw your opponent over your outstretched right leg to the mats.

There are several different variations of this counter just as you will meet different methods of strangling from the front but all can be dealt with by methods based on those just described. For example, instead of placing your right arm beneath his left and your left over his right arm and clasping your hands, you can place your right hand beneath his left elbow and press upwards and your left hand on his right elbow and press down. As before, turn to your left for a Body Drop Throw—the result will be just as effective. This latter method is perhaps more easy to operate. Of course, once you have broken your opponent's balance, you can use almost any throw provided that it is applied in the direction of his movement.

Essential Points in the Body Drop Throw as a Counter to a Strangle Hold from the Front

(*a*) Your opponent is attempting to strangle you from your front, immediately slide your right arm under his left, simultaneously slipping your left arm over his right and clasping your hands firmly together by interlacing the fingers.

(*b*) Now turn to your left by lowering and withdrawing your left hip and as you do so take your opponent round you in a circular movement to your left with your arms, your left arm continuing the downward movement and the right still pushing up.

(*c*) Continuing to turn to the left bring your leg, again controlled by the hip, across in front of him and place it lightly on the mats so that your foot, at the level of your achilles tendon, makes contact with his ankle or the lower part of his shin. Remember that your weight and balance must be completely on your left leg (Fig. 65), which should be well bent.

(*d*) Continue the turning movement until your opponent loses his balance completely and falls over your out-stretched right leg to the mats. If you find that your opponent is able to step over your right leg you can counter by raising your leg so that your foot is just below his knee, but remember that at all times it is a confession of failure and the real reason that he is able to step over your leg is that you have failed to move correctly and his balance remained unbroken.

How to Break a Strangle Hold from the Rear

There are also a variety of ways of strangling a person from behind but the only effective method is that which necessitates your opponent placing his arm round your neck and pulling you against him so that the back of your

head or neck is close against his chest (Fig. 66). To be effective a strangle hold of this type requires that your balance should be broken to the rear and therefore the main essen-tial of the counter is to recover your balance: to do this, you have to curve your body forward.

Imagine that, as is usu-ally the case, your oppon-ent is right-handed and attacks by throwing his right arm round your neck. He might do several things with his left arm but the most probable is that he will either place his left hand against the back of your head to increase his leverage or he might clasp his hands together in order to obtain the same effect.

Fig. 66

Whatever the method of attack used clasp his right arm with both your hands and pull it forwards and upwards at the same time lowering your hips. Do this by bending your knees and force your hips backwards in order to recover your own balance and break that of your opponent. As well as bringing you back on balance the grip on his arm will have the effect of relaxing the hold on your throat. Transfer your weight to your left leg and slide your right leg back so that the hollow just above your heel is against the outside of your opponent's leg, as low as possible. As you do this continue to pull his right arm forward and to your left in a circular movement with your hands and, by withdrawing your left hip, throw him over your extended right leg as in the Body Drop (Fig. 67).

There is a second popular and most effective method of countering this hold. As before you hold your opponent's right arm with your hands, pulling it forwards and upwards. Again lower your hips by bending your knees and drive them directly back into your attacker. He will now be forced to his toes and will lose all his power and effectiveness. This time, continue to push your hips back and pull forward with your hands and you will find

Fig. 67

your opponent hurled directly over your shoulder to the mats. Throw him just as you would a sack of coal by throwing him forward over your shoulder but at the same time getting your own body out of the way by turning to your left as you do so. You should as always do this by withdrawing and lowering your left hip. Take great care to maintain your balance as you make this throw as, should you fall forward, not only will you be unable to check your opponent whilst practising and assist his breakfall, but you may pitch him direct on his head and land on him yourself.

Counter to an Attack with a Stick

This is another popular counter to a very familiar method of attack. Your opponent, holding a stick in his right hand, intends to strike directly downwards (Fig. 68).

As he does so you step towards his right side with your left foot, at the same time bringing your left arm up to intercept the blow—this is also shown in Fig. 68. You must check his descending arm by catching his arm on the sharp boney side of your own forearm, but take care as you do so that the flexibility of his wrist does not allow the stick to continue its movement downwards and strike your head. If

Fig. 68

you have moved correctly, even if this follow through does occur, your head will be too far away from the stick for any contact to be possible.

When you have actually blocked his blow, bring your right arm up behind his bent arm and clasp your own left wrist with your right (Fig. 69). The resulting lock is very similar to the Figure Four Lock. Having secured this position, still keeping your body curved forward, step forward with your right foot taking your opponent's arm with you in a circular movement to his rear and downwards. You will find yourself in such a position that you have the choice of either breaking an attacker's arm or using the leverage to hurl him hard to the mats—possibly both. Take great care in practice or you might find yourself actually carrying out one of these alternatives on your unfortunate opponent. This opponent must submit in

Fig. 69

good time and you must immediately recognise his submission.

As an alternative it is just as simple to apply a Shoulder Throw as a counter to this downward blow. Again you check the blow with your left forearm but this time allow the movement of his attack to continue but guide it round you, past your left shoulder (Fig. 70). Now turn to your left by withdrawing your left hip and leg and bring your right arm over and round your opponent's right arm, using his jacket at the back of his elbow for your grip (Fig.71). As you do this, grip the sleeve of your opponent's jacket with your left hand, pulling him forward. At this stage, if you have pulled him forward, you will have obtained body contact and, by driving your hips back into him and continuing your turn to your left, you will hurl him to the mats in a shoulder throw.

Fig. 70

Fig. 71

CHAPTER XI

LESSON 10

The Hip Throw Counter to a "Bear Hug" from Behind

To the inexperienced this is one of the most hopeless positions in which it is possible to find oneself but to the experienced exponent of judo it presents few difficulties. The attacker has approached you unsuspected from the rear and has flung his arms round you. To make the

position even worse your own arms have been pinned firmly to your sides in the process and to all appearances there is little to be done except wait to be hurled to the ground at the will of your attacker (Fig. 72).

Actually, as already stated, there should be no such danger. The first move is as usual in judo to lower your hips and curve your body forward in order to secure or regain your own balance and weaken that of your

Fig. 72

opponent (Fig. 73). As you do this hunch your shoulders spreading your elbows diagonally sideways and forwards (Fig. 74) in a firm and decisive movement and thrusting your hips back into your opponent. If you have moved smoothly and correctly not only will your attacker be curved forward and come up on his toes but his grip round your arms and body will also have been broken, his arms being forced upwards towards the vicinity of your shoulders. This is the time to grip his right arm with your hands and pull it forward and upwards, simultaneously sliding your right leg back against the outside of his right ankle and throwing him by turning to your left by lowering and taking back your left hip.

Similarly you can also, if you are shorter than your opponent, throw him directly over your shoulder as shown when countering a strangle hold from the rear. It is important, whichever method you choose, to push your hips back into your opponent in the same movement as that in which you raise your elbows and hunch your shoulders. Your

Fig. 73

elbows must be raised outwards very firmly especially

Fig. 74

if the grip on your arms and body is strong. Of course, once you have carried out these movements successfully, the more your opponent strives to retain his hold, the weaker his position becomes. He should either break clear or change his form of attack so that it is transferred to the direction of your defensive movement.

COUNTERS TO BLOWS OF VARIOUS TYPES:

1. A Straight Right to the Jaw

Briefly the counter to the straight right aimed at the jaw is a Shoulder Throw, but it is not quite as simple as that for as always in judo complete control of both your own body and that of your opponent is required. Assume once more that your opponent is right-handed and attempts to strike at your jaw with his right fist. First parry the blow with your left forearm to your left and slightly upwards, gliding your left foot slightly, towards him. Immediately step in with your right foot turning it well to your left and placing it in front of the right foot of your opponent (Fig. 75). As your right foot moves in, you must draw back and lower your left hip slightly curving your

body forward. This serves the dual purpose of allowing your opponent to continue his original movement without a check and also brings you into position to follow up this movement as well as taking your head out of the line of his punch.

Now turn to your left on the ball of your right foot but keeping your balance over your left hip.

Fig. 75

Make your turn by taking the left side of your body back and round controlled by the left hip which should move first, not by advancing the right side of your body towards your opponent. As you turn, keep your body low by bending your knees and curved forward slightly and, with your left hand, guide your opponent's right arm to his front,

your right arm sliding under his right arm close to the shoulder and coming round his upper arm. Figure 75 shows the commencement of this movement. Finally, whilst keeping his right arm pulled well forward and slightly upwards, push your hip back into your opponent (Fig. 76) to bring him up on to his toes completely off balance. Then, by means of the forward pull on his arm and pushing back with your hips, you continue to turn to your left by withdrawing the left hip until you find your opponent

Fig. 76

hurled completely over your right shoulder to the mats. Don't forget to check the fall in practice.

Essential Points in the Counter to the Straight Right

1. You require complete smoothness and continuity of movement to make this counter throw really successful.

2. Do not attempt to check your opponent's right arm but rather parry his blow with your left forearm allowing his movement to continue past you and bring your right arm round the outside of his upper arm. Do not attempt to grip his arm with your right hand—you can hold it in a grip between your upper arm and forearm (Fig. 76).

3. Parry to your left and upwards, stepping in with your right foot as you do so. This right foot must be well turned to your left (Fig 75).

4. Your hips must be well lowered by bending your knees in order to bring your hips below those of your opponent. Remember that even though you bend your knees you keep your body upright except for the slight curve forward which is required for balance and strength and to break the balance of your opponent.

5. Guide your opponent's arm directly to his front and slightly upward. It must not be pulled down on to your shoulder; in fact there is no need for it to touch your shoulder at all.

6. Make the throw by pushing your hips firmly back into your opponent. As you pull his arm forward—do not attempt to lift him with your hips.

2. Counter to a Right-Hand Punch to the Stomach

Once more you are attacked, this time an attempt being made to land a right-hand punch to your stomach or possibly your chest.

The essential preliminary is to ward off the blow with your right forearm, allowing your opponent's arm to continue past your right side. As you do this, step in with

your left foot turning your body to your right (Fig. 77) by withdrawing your right hip. This also allows the blow to pass harmlessly should your warding off movement be unsuccessful. You can also help it along with your left hand on his sleeve.

As your attacker's arm passes you, maintain contact with it with your right forearm, guiding it through and bring your left hand over his

Fig. 77

upper arm, bring his arm into your arm-pit and grip his wrist with your right hand, turning further to your right by moving your right hip and foot in a circular movement to your right away from your opponent. You should finish up facing the same direction as his original blow. Press your left arm down on his elbow and push down (Fig. 78), pulling up with your right hand. At this stage the lock is applied but a sharp downward blow would have broken his arm. If instead you continue to pull his right arm to his front and hold steadily down with your left arm on his elbow you can, by lowering your hips and bending your knees, force him to the ground face down where you can drop the weight of your body on to his right shoulder and apply a

Fig. 78

final arm lock by holding him down at the shoulder with your knee and pulling up his forearm by means of your grip on his wrist with your right hand (Fig. 79.)

An alternative defence to this form of attack is to use a hip throw to your left—the normal side. In this case you ward off the blow in exactly the same manner but with your left forearm instead of your right and his blow is guided past your left side (Fig. 80). Allowing his blow to

Fig. 79

continue, you turn on your right foot by withdrawing your left hip and, as you do so, allow your right arm to come round his waist to make contact for the Hip Throw described on page 46, Fig 20.

Another alternative is to counter with a Hip Throw made to your right, what is termed a left-handed throw. This time you ward off the blow with your left forearm and having done so allow your left arm to slide along his right and round his waist (Fig. 81). Now grip his left sleeve with your right hand

Fig. 80

and turn on your right foot. Note that this is an exceptional case in which you bring your left hip in to your opponent. As you do so make your turn and pull your opponent round to your right. You will now find yourself in position to complete your left-handed hip throw by transferring all your weight to your right foot and withdrawing your right hip (Fig. 82).

Fig. 81   Fig. 82

3. Counter to Uppercut Aimed at Jaw

This is a very simple counter, easy to apply and exceedingly effective when applied smoothly and correctly. If you fail to obtain smooth movement your counter is bound to fail although it will enable you to avoid the actual blow.

As your opponent aims an uppercut at your jaw withdraw your hips away from him as far as is required actually to cause his fist to miss your stomach and jaw; if necessary take a short step back with your left foot to ensure that you do not get hit. Now as the blow passes by you harmlessly take a long smooth step in with your left foot, bringing up your left arm and catching his blow by blocking his forearm with your own left forearm but allowing and assisting its movement to continue upward (Fig. 75). Curve your body forward and push his arm on upwards and backwards in a circular movement to his rear and bring your right hand behind his arm and clasp your own left hand with your right in exactly the same way as shown in Fig. 69 on page 118. Now continue the movement to his rear, stepping past him as you do so with your right foot and you will find that his body will be bent back until the point is reached when you can either break his arm or throw him violent to the ground.

It must be noted that your opponent's arm is moved in a circular action to his rear. First it is taken upwards in continuation of his blow then it reaches its peak and continues backwards to the rear, finally moving downwards as you step in and curve your body. This circular movement must be maintained if your counter-attack is to be successful.

How to Break Grips on your Body and Clothing

Although most professional self-defence "experts" teach many methods of defence against grips on your hair, body and clothing there is actually no necessity to do so as there is one basic counter which serves all occasions if varied slightly as required.

Consider the case of the attacker who grips you by your jacket or lapel with his right hand. Do not fight to free yourself from the hold but rather place the palm of your open right hand on his to hold him in that position as you do so stepping in towards him with your left foot placing it between his feet and turning it to your right to assist your turn in that direction which follows. Your left arm is now placed over your opponent's right upper arm pressing it to your side between your upper arm and body and at the same time you turn on the ball of your left foot to your right, bending your knees and lowering your hips until you are facing the same direction as your opponent. Continue to grip his upper arm between your own left arm and body with firm pressure at the same time bending your knees more and more with your right hand pulling his arm up under your arm-pit to apply an arm lock (Fig. 78). You must keep your body upright so that the pressure on his arm is increased not so much by pulling it upwards but rather by the whole weight of your body as you lower your hips. Ensure that the thumb of his right hand is kept downward when you apply the lock in order that the pressure is against the elbow joint. If the thumb is not kept down he will be able to bend his elbow and avoid the lock.

Supposing that instead of grasping your jacket your opponent grabs your hair with his right hand. Once more place your right hand on his right hand to prevent him releasing his grip and at the same time step in with your left foot, turning to your right by taking your right hip away from him in a circular movement using the left hip as a pivot and bring your left arm up and over his right upperarm to apply an arm lock already described (Fig. 78).

How to Break a Grip on your Wrist

A hold on your wrist should at no time present any great difficulty as, provided you apply pressure to the weakest point, even a strong opponent should fail to maintain his grip. The point of attack if you are held in such a grip is the angle between your opponent's thumb and his fingers. By correct movement you are able to apply the whole power of your body against his thumb by pressing up against the angle between fingers and thumb and

Fig. 83

forcing up your forearm and driving your hand upwards (Fig. 83). If correct technique is applied there is no more in it than these simple movements but, especially in the case of a powerful attacker, judo principles require to be applied.

Assume that your right wrist is held by your opponent's right hand. At once bring your right elbow into

your body and press on the angle between his thumb and
fingers with your forearm but do so by bending your knees
and lowering your hips so that the whole body moves as
one, not as individual movement of the arms alone. Now
raise your body in a circular movement of the hips moving
into your opponent and upwards and again by moving in
one compact unit your wrist is drawn against his thumb
with the whole power of your body behind it—this is the
reason you wedge your elbow into your side—to obtain
leverage. You will find that your opponent, with only his
thumb and fingers to resist the whole power of your body,
will be absolutely unable to retain his hold, and as it is
broken, the ideal opportunity for a rear throw usually
occurs.

With a little practice you will be able to vary this
method to break holds on your wrists and arms whichever
way you are held, even if both wrists should be held
simultaneously by different opponents.

CHAPTER XII

LESSON 11

Counters to Attacks with a Knife

Without any doubt whatsoever the best method of defending yourself against a knife attack is not to get into a position where such a defence becomes necessary, but should self-defence become essential against an armed aggressor, there is no doubt that the trained judo exponent should stand a very good chance of coming out safely, and a far better chance than any man unversed in the art of judo.

You will remember that self-defence is based on the basic principles of judo so for that reason you will find that these counters against knife attacks are very similar to throws and locks already described.

The first defence is that used against a straight thrust at your chest or stomach with a knife and is similar to that for a punch (Fig. 77). Of course at first the main consideration is not to apply a counter but to avoid the thrust and for this reason you turn your hips to the right, assisting this movement by stepping forward with the left foot, advancing the left hip and drawing back the right. This allows the knife to pass harmlessly but to ensure that it does so, you push the attacker's forearm away to your right with your own right forearm with your hand down and if you ward off the blow with a sharp cutting movement from the boney part of your forearm the pain will probably disarm him (Fig. 77). Now that the immediate danger has passed the time has come to apply a counter. Grip the attacker's wrist or forearm with your right hand by sliding it over his arm and help it to continue in the direction of its thrust, at the same time you should make a turn to your right pivoting on the ball of your left foot and bringing your left hand down on your opponent's right elbow to disable it. Alternatively, if you wish you can continue the pull to his front with your right arm and maintain the downward pressure with your left until he is forced to the ground where you can finish him with a blow or an arm lock or simply disarm him (Fig. 79).

At first you may find it difficult to grasp your opponent's right arm after you have parried his blow. Actually it is quite simple if you parry with your right arm so turned that you use the sharp edge of your forearm with your palm turned towards you, fingers downward. Now you should find it easy to slip your hand over the top of his arm and obtain a grip. Even should you still find this difficult at first, practise will overcome the problem.

An alternative counter to this form of attack is to use a Hip Throw. Step in with your left foot and parry his arm with your left forearm, to your left. You will find that your step in and the momentum provided by his own effort, will bring him close to you and you will be in an ideal position to slip your left arm round his waist, pivot on your right foot, to your right and apply a hip throw on the reverse side. Similarly a hip counter to the normal side, turning to your left, can be used.

Counter to a Disembowelling Stroke with a Knife

In this form of attack your opponent brings his knife upwards in an attempt to drive it into your stomach. This time check his attack by blocking his right forearm with the sharp boney edge of your left forearm (Fig. 84) at the same time stepping forward with your left foot. His thrust is checked but the movement of his body allowed to continue to your left side. As this happens grip his right sleeve above the elbow with your right hand and moving in with your right foot past his right side, turn on the ball of that foot to your right, bringing his arm up behind his back

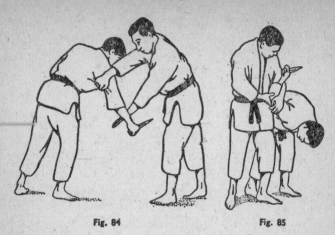

Fig. 84   Fig. 85

into a "Hammer Lock" (Fig. 85). Your feet should now be in line and facing in the same direction as those of your opponent (Fig. 85).

You should have your left arm under his right and place your left hand near his right shoulder. Your right hand continues to control his elbow but you now have him helpless in the arm lock and can disarm him with ease as you are able to maintain the hold with your left arm alone, the right now being free (see Fig. 85).

Counter to a Downward Thrust with a Knife—2

A very common form of attack either as a blow or particularly, with a stick, this is also a usual but unwise method of using a knife and is actually the most easy to counter.

As your opponent strikes down with his right hand you parry with your left forearm against his forearm stepping forward as you do so with your left foot (Fig. 68). Now by using the momentum of your movement, take his arm up and to his rear, bringing your right arm up behind his arm and clasping your left wrist with your right to apply the arm lock (Fig. 69).

Alternatively, you can parry his blow with your right

Fig. 86   Fig. 87

forearm (Fig. 86) and then step in behind him and apply a strangle hold from the rear (Fig. 87) or use your advantage in many different ways, depending on your own personal preference and, even more important, depending on which movement comes naturally to you at the time.

Counter-attacks in Judo—General Principles

As you must have realised it is impossible to teach any definite counter to a particular throw because although you might have seen a series of throws and counters performed by Black Belt holders at some judo display, these are not laid down as set moves to be made in any certain circumstances, but are rather correct basic movements based on the throw or counter throw which most suits their particular style and the style of their opponent.

On no occasion will a good judo man be heard to say that any particular method is correct and all others wrong, for provided that your movements fit in with the principle of judo, "maximum efficiency—minimum effort" the most effective method is the one that best suits you.

If you wish to attain a high grade there are a few basic rules which must be observed as they are necessary to apply effective throws and counter throws. You must control your body from your abdomen and hips, for you will find that when you move your hips the rest of your body follows thus enabling you to move as one complete unit. Should you move your shoulder first it is impossible to move the rest of your body in conjunction with it and therefore your movement becomes disjointed and ineffective. For this reason you can with practice recover your balance, when an effort is made to throw you, by moving your hips and transferring your balance to another point with the result that your opponent has to all intents or purposes attacked in the wrong direction. This is one of the reasons why the judo man must move with his body upright and relaxed in order that his weight and balance can be transferred instantly in any direction as required.

Another point to note is that to effect a throw your opponent must usually position himself so that his hips are below yours—in other words his centre of balance is below your own. This means that if you are moving correctly with your body upright and relaxed you can lower your hips by bending your knees and thus make it impossible for your opponent to get his hips below yours and effect his throw but you must not maintain this position as a throw cannot be made from it—it is only a counter or defensive measure.

It is very often possible to avoid a Hip Throw, Body Drop or any type of throw which entails your opponent turning away from you by dropping your left hand from the lapel to his hip using it against his body at hip level to check his turn. This makes him hesitate in the middle of his move and leaves an opening for you to place your left arm around his waist and effect a Hip Throw to your right, the opposite side to that described in the chapter on Hip Throws (Fig. 88). This is one of the most popular counters in judo and also illustrates the important fact that to avoid throws, just as to keep out of difficulty in groundwork, you must not only be able to move your hips freely but must have control of your opponent's hips.

Fig. 88

In theory of course if a throw is carried out correctly, with your opponent's balance broken, your own balance maintained and your movements made smoothly and in the correct direction, there is no question that you will make your throw with no danger of a counter being applied against you. The danger arises because we seldom carry out all these items successfully. Whenever a move is made, or even the preliminary movement for a throw, one must to a certain extent sacrifice one's safe defensive posture and, unless the opponent's position and balance are disturbed to a far greater degree than the attacker sacrifices his own there can be a counter throw. If you lose your own balance you will fail to make your throw, even though it is not certain that a counter will succeed. It is surprising how often in judo a man comes in for a throw and if it were not for his grip on his opponent's jacket would himself fall over due to his bad balance.

Accurate judgment of the direction of your opponent's movement is also extremely important. However well his balance is broken, if the throw is attempted against his natural movement, only extreme physical strength will bring off a throw and if such an effort is used against an experienced exponent of judo the resulting counter will be sudden and painful. You will have observed how in every throw it was emphasised that the thrower moves in a circle even though the circle is described in various directions for the different throws. Should this circle be broken before the throw is completed, then that throw should be a failure and open to counter. This is clearly illustrated in a Drawing Ankle Throw in which you step back to your right rear bringing your opponent round you in a circular movement to your left. If at any time that circle to your left, actually a circle described round your right hip, should be broken your opponent will be able to step in and apply a counter throw and even if he is not sufficiently experienced to do this at least he will have no difficulty in avoiding your effort.

In practice and contests you must watch for these breaks in the rhythm of your opponent's movement and take advantage of them. When he makes an attempt to throw, you should avoid it by control of movement of your hips—which also has the effect of breaking up his circular movement and leaving him open for your counter-attack. This will be demonstrated in the descriptions of counters to certain throws which follow.

Counter to a Hip Throw

The Hip Throw is the most popular of all throws in judo with all grades from White to Black Belt. Although it has many variations the methods of dealing with it and making counters are similar in all cases and, like the throw itself, the counter is one of those most commonly seen on the judo mat. When your opponent moves in to throw you with a Hip Throw on the normal side, that is he turns to his left attempting to break your balance to your right, bend your knees slightly and move your hips forward to retain your balance and upright posture, at the same time check his turning movement by placing your left hand on his right hip (Fig. 88), at the same time moving your left foot and hip to your left rear in order to break up the strong forward curve of his body. No force is required and it is only necessary to place your hand on his hip for an instant to break up his circular movement. Immediately you feel him check, take your left hand from his hip and slide it round his waist and turn to your right on the ball of your right foot, bringing your left hip through so that you are in a position to effect a hip

throw on the reverse side (Fig. 89). You can also check him by checking his right shoulder with your left hand but this is not so effective as it has no control of his hips.

Fig. 89

The secret of this counter is to make use of your opponent's original movement. For this reason you must only check him for a moment with your left hand whilst you transfer your balance, then you allow him to continue. In fact you require his momentum to assist you make your throw. All you do is to place your hips in the way and in his efforts to throw you he will hurl himself over them.

Counter to Shoulder Throw

Although it is possible to use the counter just described for a Hip Throw in reply to a Shoulder Throw it is far more difficult and there is another counter which is just as effective and more easy to apply. The counter that is about to be described can be used against a Hip Throw although it requires slight modification.

Immediately you sense the first sign of your opponent

attempting a Shoulder Throw you must take counter measures. As he turns to his left bringing his right arm or elbow under and round your right arm he has to bend his knees in order to lower his hips sufficiently to get his shoulder beneath your arm and his hip below yours—this is the weak point in the throw and is your opportunity to apply the counter. Drop your left hand from your opponent's lapel and place it in the small of his back, using sufficient pressure to bend his body backwards

Fig. 90

thus breaking his balance to the rear (Fig. 90), moving your balance to your left rear as you do so as in the Hip Throw Counter. At this stage, pivot to your left on the ball of your right foot and withdraw your left hip to your left. You must take your left foot off the mat and make at least a complete quarter turn to your left taking your opponent with you. As you have already broken his balance to his rear he will be unable to turn with you and will be hurled on his back to the mats. Alternatively you could step back and strangle your opponent with your right arm (Fig. 66).

In this counter throw, it is important that as you turn to your left you take your opponent with you, although this is actually made rather more difficult by the fact that your left hand is resting on your opponent's back. The control must come from your right hand which, as has so often been emphasised, follows exactly the course described by your left hip as it is withdrawn. Also it is essential to take your left foot off the mat and move it, together with your body, in a complete turn to your left— the further you turn, the more effective will be the throw. If you react sufficiently rapidly, you can perform this counter without moving the grip of your left hand from your opponent's lapel but this, as a movement, requires a great deal of skill and experience.

Counter to a Major Outer Reaping Throw

A very popular throw, the Major Outer Reaping, appears to leave itself more open to a counter than most throws. This is not actually the case and the impression is given by the fact that as it is a throw made to an opponent's rear it should only be used when it is possible to break his balance in that direction. Unfortunately, this is frequently forgotten, with the result that instead of successfully completing a throw you sacrifice your own posture and leave yourself open to what is not so much a counter as another Major Outer Reaping in its own right.

The time to attempt to counter the Major Outer Reaping is as your opponent steps past you on your right with his left foot whilst attempting to break your balance to your rear. Immediately react by drawing your hips back to recover your balance, and you should find yourself in a strong position with your hips drawn back and your body curved slightly forward and your opponent, as a result of your hip movement, having to reach forward with his right leg to make his throw. He is unable to do this unless he inclines his body to his rear and this is exactly the position in which he attempted to place you. At once glide forward with your left foot to his right side, keeping his body inclined to his rear and breaking his balance completely in that direction with a downward turn of your wrists. Now bring your right hip and leg forward and thrust it back to sweep his right leg away from him, throwing him to his back to the mats. In effect you have brought off against him exactly the same throw he tried on you. Further details can be found in the lesson dealing with the Major Outer Reaping itself on page 70.

When avoiding this type of throw, it is essential that the movement of your hips away from your opponent is

instantaneous—in fact it must be instinctive—you have
no time to think. Also, should you find that, having
avoided the throw, you are unable to break his balance to
the rear, do not attempt to effect the counter throw—
remember that there are always counters to counter
throws.

CHAPTER XIII

LESSON 12

The Spring Hip Throw

This is probably the most beautiful and one of the most difficult throws in judo. It is exacting in that it demands a combination of almost perfect timing, complete control of both your own and your opponent's balance and close body contact. The basic form of the throw is made when your opponent's legs are fairly straight and his balance is brought forward. This is the throw which is described first.

It is essential to bring your opponent's chest into close contact with your own and this should be done as you withdraw your left hip turning to your left. Assuming the normal hold and position, step back with your left foot, placing it on the mat so that it is behind your right forming a 'T' at the same time lifting him with your wrists shaped like the neck of a swan and pulling him forward until his chest and yours come into close contact (Fig. 91). At this stage, because of the contact, he is turned with you as you move. Your left knee must be well bent to bring your hips below your opponent's hips. On no account must you move back into your opponent—you must bring him into you. These preliminary

Fig. 91

movements are shown in Fig. 91. Maintaining the contact continue to turn pivoting on your left foot and bringing up your right leg so that it contacts your opponent across both his legs just below his knee (Fig. 92). Press back on to your opponent with your right leg, continuing to pull him up and into you with your hands and continuing

to turn. At this stage, lean forward and he will be lifted off the mats by your right leg and then thrown off it to the mats (Fig. 92).

Fig. 92

Essential Points in the Spring Hip Throw

(a) Bring your opponent into firm chest contact with you with a lift and pull of your wrists, as you do so taking back your left hip and placing your left foot on the mat behind your right in the form of a 'T' but turning it as far to the left as possible to avoid losing your balance at the final phase of the throw. Your knees must be bent as much as possible.

(b) Place the lower part of your right leg across both your opponent's legs just below his knees pressing it firmly back against him.

(c) Lean forward by bending your left knee and by pressing your right leg back you will lift your opponent off the mats without effort.

(d) As he lifts continue to turn to your left and he will be "sprung off" your right leg to the mats—hence the name of the throw.

(e) Impetus can be added to the throw by straightening your left leg in the last movement (d) above.

Variation of the Spring Hip Throw

The formal version of the throw just described is extremely difficult to perform successfully, so much so that the large majority of attempts not only fail but are countered owing to the necessity to turn so far whilst balanced, or perhaps unbalanced would be more correct, on one leg. For this reason it has never become a popular contest throw. There is however an alternative version of the throw which, whilst not so graceful and spectacular, is far more easy to perform and not so open to counter.

The preliminary movement is exactly the same, close contact and withdrawal of the left hip and leg, but it is not quiet so essential to turn the left foot so far to the left although it is to be preferred. In this version, the right foot is only lifted slightly catching the inside of your opponent's leg as low down as possible with the outside of your leg and pressing firmly back and outwards (Fig. 93). Lean forward to obtain the lift and make the throw by turning. This will, as before, ensure that your opponent is thrown off your right leg.

Fig. 93

The great advantage of this method is that it is not necessary to sink so low as your left leg or turn so far to your left with the result that time is saved and it is easier to maintain balance. As part of your pressure with your right foot is outward it is far more difficult for your opponent to move to his left or rear to counter. Briefly this may be described as the contest version of the Spring Hip Throw.

Variations of the Shoulder Throw

In the lesson on the Shoulder Throw on page 57, it was pointed out that it is a short man's throw or at least, because it is essential to maintain your balance forward, it is a throw which is carried out against a taller opponent. Whilst this is true of the basic throw, it does not apply to certain variations of the throw, two of which I propose to describe.

1—The Winding Shoulder Throw

This is the favourite throw of the writer, who is rather tall to apply the normal throw against the average opponent. Carried out against an opponent whose balance is forward, the throw requires that your opponent's balance is broken to his right front. This position can be obtained by means of an upward turn of the wrists and withdrawal of the left hip. When the balance is broken, continue the turn and pull of the left hand, transferring the right hand from your opponent's left

Fig. 94

to right lapel where it drives upwards and in the direction of the turn following the pull of your left hand (Fig. 94). You can sweep with your right leg to maintain contact.

At this stage when your right hand is driving upwards, continue your turn, curving your body forward and pushing your hips backward into your opponent. As you turn, he will be wound over your hip, the contact automatically becoming closer and closer the more you turn until he is finally hurled completely over your hips or shoulder.

Another advantage of this throw is that if your opponent defends by bending his knees and leaning backwards, you can completely change the direction of your throw and bring off a leg wheel to his right side or even a Major Outer Reaping to his rear.

2—The Shoulder Drop

This throw is not as widely used as the Shoulder or Hip Throw but is equally effective and has the added advantage that it may be performed to your opponent's front or side according to the direction of his movement. It is effective against an opponent considerably shorter than yourself and therefore has certain advantages over the Shoulder Throw.

In this lesson, the throw to your opponent's front will be described, that to the side being a simple variation and, in any case, it is a useful exercise to develop movements for yourself.

This is another throw made when your opponent's legs are fairly straight and his balance is forward. Wait until he steps forward with his right foot and, by pulling in the direction of his step and lifting with your left hand and at the same time withdrawing your left hip, you can effectively break his balance to his right front. Your right hand and arm as usual push to your left following the direction taken by your left hip. The left hip should be dropped by bending your knee as you turn and immediately your opponent's balance is broken, release your right hand and bring it through, passing it under and round your opponent's right upper arm to clasp his sleeve near

his right elbow (Fig. 95). As your turn continues you
should bring your left elbow
down towards your left knee
and you will find his right arm
is allowed to slide down the
outside of your right arm into
the crook of your right elbow
if it did not get there in the
preliminary movement. Your
right arm now assists to pull
your opponent forward so
that you have contact with
him. Simultaneously with the

Fig. 95

change of grip you should drop your right leg back as
in the Body Drop to trap his right foot and prevent his
recovery by stepping forward. Your continuing turn
throws him over your outstretched right leg (Fig. 94).

There are rather a large number of movements in this
throw and a summary is required, but it must be remembered that so many of the movements take place together
or merge in to each other that it is essential that the
throw is taken movement by movement for training
purposes only.

(a) As your opponent steps forward, turn to your left
lowering your left hip and taking him with you.

(b) Continue to turn, bringing your left elbow down
towards your left knee and changing the hold of your
right hand, bringing it under and round his right arm
which is brought down into the crook of your elbow.

(c) Continuing to turn and pull him forward, drop
back your right foot to trap his right. Your continued
turn will throw him over your leg.

CHAPTER XIV

LESSON 13

General Notes on Balance and Movement

Although every effort has been made in this book to describe and teach the basic forms of the throws, holds and locks and avoid variations except where stated, I do not suggest that readers should follow the lessons blindly. Movements, particularly throws, will have to be varied according to your build and that of your opponent, and more and wider variations can be made as you progress. This applies particularly to your hold on your opponent's jacket. A successful throw must be always effortless and unless it is so, a change is required at some stage—in other words let your test be

"Maximum efficiency—minimum effort."

If this test applies, your movement is good judo—if it does not, it is not.

If the reader is particularly strong or heavy, it will be far more difficult for him to form honest judgment but experience and even better a qualified instructor will soon show him the way provided he is willing to give up what may at present be proving very effective methods as a result of superior strength to adopt a style which is probably for the time being far less effective. It does not matter how often you are thrown attempting to achieve results by correct methods as in grading contests promotion is awarded more on style and the movements that are attempted than on actual results. Later of course, correct efforts will produce effective results.

Incidentally, never refuse in practice to allow yourself to be thrown if the throw is almost there. Resistance can result in accidents caused by the thrower falling on his opponent. In any case, breakfalls require practice as much as any other form of judo and this is a good opportunity to obtain this practise.

Two points have been repeated constantly throughout this book, turn the foot on which you have balanced yourself as far to your left as possible (for throws to your left) and drop your hips by bending your knees. It is essential to turn your foot to the left as far as possible and to exaggerate the movement in practise. If the foot is not turned sufficiently, you will reach a stage during the throw when your body locks and your movement can only be continued by leaning back. This is fatal and should always result in a counter against you. The second point is equally vital. To make your throws effective you must attack your opponent between his knees and hips (for throws in the hip and shoulder group). If you attack too low, that is, below his knees, he can bend his knees, thus escaping your attack. If, on the other hand, your attack is aimed above his hips, he can lean back from the hips and avoid the throw.

Although your body must be kept upright when you attack, it should be curved forward slightly as if you were bowing to your opponent. By means of this curve you can apply the whole power of your body to the throw, pressing up from the mat from your toes. Failure to do this often results in lack of contact and again offers the opportunity for a counter throw.

Movement and Tactics—General Principles

If you have thoroughly worked through these pages of description and instruction of the various movements you will have formed a very sound idea of what judo is all about. In theory, it ought to be possible to perform these movements smoothly, gracefully and, above all, effectively. Unfortunately, this is seldom possible and although the reader can perform the throws (the throws are the most important and difficult part of judo) with a co-operative partner, resistance, even to a light degree, upsets the rhythm and often either results in a failure or, even more discouraging, a counter being applied. This indicates that the danger point of judo has been reached. At this stage, figures taken from the beginners' classes of various clubs show that out of every twenty who commence, only about ten are still practising after the end of the course, whilst a further year sees only at the most five survivors. Fortunately these five are always very keen and get to the stage where they live for judo and their club.

A second danger period arises rather surprisingly at about the Blue or Brown Belt stage. Up to this grade promotion comes to the average pupil fairly auto-matically as all that is required is a smooth movement and fairly sound theory of the throws and groundwork—actual effectiveness counts for very little although it is not to be depreciated. Now the pupil approaches the final ambition of all judo enthusiasts; he is close to joining the few who hold the highly coveted Black Belt of Dan Grade. It may take as much as a year or even longer to rise from the Blue of 2nd Kyu to the Brown of 1st Kyu and even practising on three or four evenings each week another year is not unusual between Brown (1st Kyu) and Black Belt (1st Dan). There is as much difference between Brown Belt grade and 1st Dan Black Belt as there is between a beginner and Brown Belt and this is very hard for a beginner to believe when he remembers how easily a Brown Belt can handle him on the mat. It is these long gaps between promotions after quite possibly having risen through White, Yellow, Orange and Green to Blue in perhaps twelve months which cause this large percentage of comparatively experienced judo exponents to drop out at this stage.

Fortunately in a club it is often possible for an experienced, thoughtful and considerate Dan Grade instructor to cut down these periods between grades. If the instructor is alert and keen to see his pupils progress he will see basic faults in technique which are usually the cause of the hold-up. Sometimes it is only one single fault which makes the pupils' efforts fail and the pupil may even know that fault and be unable to overcome it. However, by observation and practice with him and by making thoughtful suggestions, the instructor should be able to eliminate the error and obtain the greatest pleasure that is possible to obtain from teaching—to see his pupil reach Dan Grade. This lesson therefore consists of general hints and advice on typical points which an instructor might expect to see and correct during a club's practice evening.

In throws of the hip and shoulder group it will be remembered that the hips are thrust back into the opponent to bring him to his toes for the final movement of the throw. Simple as this sounds, it is a very common source of error and the reason for a great number of failures. It must be emphasised that you thrust your hips straight back into your opponent; you must not lift with this hip action as immediately you do so your opponent has only to lift his right leg really high to be able to slide round you to your right and out of the throw. There is another important point here; if your opponent is heavy or should the thrower be light or perhaps a woman or boy, he or she will be unable to lift and will usually abandon this type of throw as far too difficult although the actual reason for these failures is not the difficulty of the throw but the failure to grasp a quite simple theoretical detail which is difficult to put into practice.

It is usually better to move away from your opponent when you attempt a throw. Although this point has been stressed several times already, it is sufficiently vital to be worthy of endless repetition. It is obvious that if you attack by moving into your opponent, it is comparatively simple for him either to stop you with his hand on your hip or to move away from you as you move in. The solution is to move yourself away from him and this is the only course open against a strong or heavy opponent.

Imagine your own body to be a door. You are about to attempt a Hip Throw to your left so your left hip must be the door itself. Now to effect the throw, the door must be opened away from your opponent and this is carried out by moving your left hip back away from him and taking the remainder of your body with it, revolving your body round and away from your right hip e.g. the door (your body) has now been opened and of course revolves on its hinges (your right hip). Naturally you must take your opponent with you as you move and by this means, after some experience has been obtained, you will be able to effect your throws against even the strongest and heaviest opponents.

The rule about keeping your opponent facing you is one of the essentials of making successful throws although you finish with your back to your opponent in some throws.

It is also one of the basic defensive measures to remain facing your opponent and a short explanation should make the reason for this quite clear. If you stand facing your opponent using a normal hold and then decide to attempt a throw, it is useless to move your own body into position for that throw if you leave your opponent undisturbed; by doing this, you merely destroy your own balance whilst leaving his balance undisturbed. You must move your whole body as one unit and thus take him round with you as you move by use of your arms—the arms moving as part of the whole body, not as separate units. The secret of judo throws is simply to disturb your opponent's balance and make him move his body but as he does so to leave your foot, leg, or hip in his way and make him fall over it as he attempts to recover.

Contact must be maintained, not only throughout actual throws but continually from the moment you take hold on your opponent's jacket. Success or failure in this respect is one of the chief reasons for promotion in grade or victory in contests.

This is a very difficult point to explain and demonstrate on the mat and much more so to put into words and for that reason great patience and experience will be required before full understanding is obtained. Take a normal hold with well relaxed arms on your opponent's jacket and keeping your elbows fairly well spread, let your hands retain their contact against your opponent's body by their own weight alone. In other words if it were not for your hold on his jacket your arms would fall to your sides. Now move away from your opponent and see what is almost certain to happen—you will pull his jacket away from his body until all the looseness is taken up—you have lost contact on his body even though you have retained hold on his jacket. If at this stage you attempt a throw you must first take up this "looseness" of the jacket before your movement affects your opponent's balance and in this space of time, short as it is, you should be countered. If contact is maintained your slightest move affects him and for this vital reason you must practise keeping the contact until you can do so continually simply by the use of the weight of your arms —but do not pull down on his jacket. If you practise with a really high grade Black Belt you will find that from the moment he takes hold on your jacket you are off balance—this is because he has "contact" and his slightest move, controlled from his hip, affects you.

There is no fixed rule about the hold on the jacket and it is difficult to find two instructors with the same opinion. Almost all the clubs affiliated to the British Judo

Association use the normal hold, left hand on opponent's sleeve and right on his lapel, but there is much more to the hold than this. This hold has developed after hundreds of years judo experience and there is a definite reason for it. The normal hold is used because most people are right-handed and naturally throw to their left and it is designed for throws in this direction and defence against similar attacks. Your left hand controls your opponent's right elbow. If he pulls or pushes you with this arm you can break up his movement by checking his elbow in any direction and, as he is usually right-handed, that is a very important point in your own defence. A hold lower down or higher up his arm, especially the latter reduces the effect. A few minutes experiment will make this obvious.

Your right hand is on your opponent's lapel and you must remember that the function of this arm in a throw to your left is to drive his body exactly in the same circular line taken by your own hips and left arm. For this reason, maximum contact and leverage are required. If your hold is too high on the lapel your hand will slip loosely round his neck where it is impossible to maintain contact and thus the throw results in failure. If you hold the lapel too far down you are getting too near his point of balance and will be exerting your effort against unnecessary opposition. Again the throw will probably fail although this latter fault of too low a grip is by far the lesser of the two. The ideal hold on the lapel is level with your own chest.

Possibly you are left-handed or you may very wisely decide that you would like to learn to effect your throws equally well on either side of your opponent. Here lies a great difficulty, for not only is throwing to your left natural to a right-handed person but even if you happen to be left-handed the normal hold which you have been taught to use is designed for throws to the left and requires modification for the reverse direction.

It is obvious, for example, that if you use a crow-bar to

lift any heavy object, the longer the bar, within reason, the greater the leverage you can exert. If you use a short bar or hold too far down the handle you will find your leverage insufficient and no amount of exertion will avail. Your hold on your opponent's jacket operates on similar lines. If you use the normal hold your grip on the sleeve with your left hand is as far out to your opponent's left as it can be with comfort—it is at the correct end of the lever, but if you attempt to throw to your right with a normal hold, your right hand grip is on your opponent's lapel, much too far down the crowbar for maximum effort— you will have to change your hold. Methods of doing this with as little warning as possible must be left to you but the vital principle to observe is obtain maximum leverage at all times.

Relaxation of mind and body are essential to good judo and can only come from considerable—many years— experience. First consider the body—if you move with a stiff body and arms, the usual attitude adopted by beginners as it prevents their being thrown by other beginners, you are unable to make a throw other than that suited to your actual fixed position and your opponent will expect and probably counter that throw. To make any other movement requires relaxing your body to change position and then, when that position is obtained, once more making your body one compact unit—not rigid—to make the throw. This can only be achieved some time after the opening to make that throw has passed. Similarly you must be close to your opponent and if you are not relaxed you may find that you are too far away, and although it may prevent you being thrown, you will also be unable to throw for the same reason and thus you will never learn judo—never really enjoy your practice. After all being thrown does not matter and it is just as great a thrill to be thrown cleanly as it is to bring off a good throw.

Equally important is to go on to the mat with your mind relaxed. It is useless to start a practice with the firm intention to bring off one throw or to have the fixed idea to dodge your opponent's favourite move. One day you will meet someone you do not know and will have no idea how to tackle him and will fall easy prey to his attack. You must relax your mind so that you react instinctively to an opening and apply counters without thought. Really good judo exponents do not know what throws they have brought off in a contest or practice—they have been part of their natural movement and have fitted into the movement of their opponent.

The Reverse Scarf Hold

Because of the comfortable position and effortless ease with which this hold can be maintained it is often called the "Arm Chair" hold. It is a good variation of the Upper Four Quarter Hold and is easy to slip into when you are in danger of having that hold broken but it is also easy to obtain from a kneeling position at the side of your opponent.

The theory is similar to that of the Scarf Hold but this time you face your opponent's feet (Fig. 96). You recline

Fig. 96

with your right hip on the mat at your opponent's left side, your legs well apart with your left as far back as

possible and the right thrown well forward. Your left arm
slips under your opponent's left arm-pit and grips the
sleeve of his jacket or even better slip it through even
further and hold the jacket at the back of his right
shoulder. Your right arm grips his belt at his right side
with your forearm pressed hard against his body, your

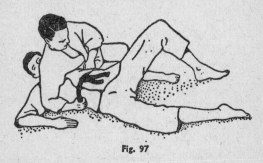

Fig. 97

elbow being pressed into his right arm-pit (Fig. 97). There
is a grave danger of your face and head receiving painful
injuries from your opponent's knees in his struggles to
free himself and it is essential that you either keep your
head well back or pressed hard down on your opponent's
body. One method is as good as the other. Figures
96 and 97 show the head held fairly well up which is
the method I adopt. Your right hip must remain in firm
contact with the side of your opponent's body throughout.

The key points to the hold are the grip of your left foot
on the mats and the hold of right hand on the belt which
must prevent him bridging or lifting his body (see methods
of escape which follow). If he does succeed in raising his
hips and attempts a backward roll his movement can be
prevented with downward pressure of your head on his
body and forward pressure from your left foot. If
necessary scissor your legs, turning on to your stomach
with a movement of the hips. This method also applies to
the Scarf Hold.

Methods of Escape from the Reverse Scarf Hold

This is probably the most difficult of all holds to break especially as it is so easy to change it to a Side Four Quarter or Upper Four Quarter Hold by scissoring your legs as just described. The main essential is to get "out of line" with your opponent so that you can escape the downward pressure of his head and lessen the effectiveness of his controlling left foot. To do this, you must at once obtain control of your opponent's hips in order to prevent him following your movements and then move your body to your right until he is no longer able to apply his head down against you. Immediately bring back your legs and hip as if attempting a backward roll and when your body is doubled up and on the point of rolling backwards, bring your left hip down and back, thus turning your body over

Fig. 98

in the air so that your legs come down toes first as if you were face down (Fig. 98). If this movement is timed correctly, you will find that not only have you turned your own body but that your momentum and hold on your opponent's hips have turned him over and only a slight adjustment is required to give you an Upper Four Quarter Hold on him.

You can also escape by moving to your left instead of right and rolling back. This method may be found easier but it depends mainly on the actual position and movements of the person holding you.

Broken Upper Four Quarter Hold

An extremely effective hold which is increased in value when applied in conjunction with the Reserve Scarf is the Broken Upper Four Quarters which has advantages over the "basic" form version of the hold being harder to break as the left (or right on the reverse side) arm is securely pinned.

The position is similar to the Upper Four Quarter but this time your left arm comes over your opponent's left arm, passing underneath his arm-pit and taking a firm grip on his collar or the back of his jacket behind his right shoulder. Your right arm goes over his right and grips his belt at his side or even better behind him, your

Fig. 99

right elbow pressing up into his arm-pit (Fig. 99). It is essential to place your right arm over his right shoulder as otherwise he can turn to his left and escape. The weight of your chest is dropped on to his left shoulder and left side of his chest, your body lying at an angle to his (Fig. 99). Your hips must be placed firmly on the mats with your legs well apart and your toes dug into the mats.

Retaining Holds on the Ground

Let it be said at once that a hold once it begins to slip should always be released and the holder either regain his feet or change to another hold or form of attack, as convenient. Usually when breaking a hold, the effort leaves you open to other attacks such as another hold or an arm lock. This has to be watched and precautions taken. Remember the three rules which must be observed in all forms of groundwork but apply to Hold Downs in particular. They are well worth repeating and are as follows.

(a) Keep your mind and body completely relaxed.

(b) Keep your hips down on the mats, and

(c) Apply your weight against your opponent's centre of balance (the part of the body which he is attempting to lift).

In importance they should be taken in this order for for there is no point in applying your weight against your opponent's body as he attempts to rise if the first rules are not followed, you will only be thrown off as you do so. Similarly it is impossible to keep your hips on the mat if your body is not relaxed.

Relaxation only becomes possible with confidence and constant practice but it is essential if immediate reaction to your opponent's struggles is to be made without the danger of being thrown off in the direction in which you apply your effort to retain your position. If you are relaxed you will be able to change from one hold to another without the necessity to overcome your opponent's effort by force—a method which always results in disaster.

The necessity of keeping your hips in contact with the mats is far more easy to explain than it is to carry out. It is obvious that if your hips remain on the mats it is impossible for your opponent to throw you over his body. In addition your weight together with your hold on his jacket prevents him moving the side of his body which is against your hips. Thus he is unable to move in either direction. On the other hand, once he is able to make you stiffen your body, you are unable to react to his movements or keep your hips on the mats and as a result you will find your hold broken.

Providing you observe the first two rules, the third should offer no great difficulty. Assume for example a Side Four Quarter Hold on your opponent's right side (Fig. 49 on page 87). You are attempting to hold your opponent who tries to sit up. This is easily countered by pressing with the toes of your right foot and pulling him down with your left hand. An effort to lift the hips is prevented by pressure from the toes of your left foot together with a pull from your right hand. Should you find him withdrawing his right hip, pull him into you with your hands and press down with your chest. Finally, should he try to turn to his left, the weight of your hips on the mat will prevent the movement.

One final point, never hesitate to change your form of attack. If your opponent begins to succeed in his efforts to withdraw his right hip and turns on his right side to escape your Side Four Quarter Hold, slip your right hand from between his legs and grip the left side of his belt at the same time bring up your right knee, controlling it from your hip and sliding your knee across his body as near his waist as possible to come astride him (Fig. 55 on page 94). It may be necessary to lift yourself with your left knee as you do so. This leaves you in a position to attack with strangle or arm locks or to move across his body to hold him from his left side. There is another alternative, a very little known but extremely effective hold—The Reverse Upper Four Quarter.

The Reverse Upper Four Quarters Hold Down

This hold is remarkable for its extreme simplicity and the fact that it is very rarely used. Its great advantages are the openings for arm locks it leaves even when the hold itself fails and that it does not leave you in a position of disadvantage should it fail or be broken.

To attempt the hold it is necessary to get into a position astride your opponent with your knees well up into his arm-pits. In this hold it is impossible to place your hips on the mats but they are dropped relaxed on your opponent's body as high up as possible. Your right arm (or you can of course reverse the hold) is placed under your opponent's arm and then grips the back of his jacket or collar as far

Fig. 100

over as possible, behind his left shoulder is ideal (Fig. 100). Your legs are pressed against the sides of his body to prevent him turning and the upper part of your body is thrown forward with your hand stretched forward on the mat. This hand can be moved to either side in order to enable you to maintain you balance (Fig. 100).

In his efforts to break this hold, your opponent is almost certain to roll over, which gives you a strangle hold, or to push up at your chest or shoulders, which leaves him open to various arm locks.

Final Notes on Groundwork

Before leaving groundwork finally there are one or two useful points which will increase the effectiveness of this side of your judo. The first concerns general movement on the ground, the art of "giving way" or offering no resistance. If you attempt to retain a hold by resisting your opponent's push against you, you turn your attack

into a trial of strength and stand to lose either against
opponents who are stronger or more skilful. A typical
example is the method of avoiding being thrown off a
hold of the Side Four Quarter type. If your opponent
manages to get his arms under your hips he can place
his elbow on the ground and obtain considerable
leverage. If you attempt to maintain your position you
will probably be thrown off. The correct answer to this
move is to give way. Using the pressure on the mats from
your toes, lift your body to the full extent of your

Fig. 101

opponent's push, thus giving him nothing against which
to use his strength (Fig. 101). Whilst he keeps on pushing
you have nothing to fear as he can take no other action
at the same time. Immediately he brings his arm down
again follow it with your hips and resume your hold. This
action can be repeated as often as he pushes and will
soon exhaust him.

The second point to remember is that a leg is always
stronger than an arm and just as you should avoid
opposing a leg with your arm you should always attempt
to apply your leg against your opponent's body. This is
very difficult at first if not impossible as your body is by no
means sufficiently supple to permit the movement. For
example, you attempt a strangle from the rear such as
shown in Fig. 24 on page 56—but your opponent manages

to lower his chin and turn his head a little and thus relieve the pressure across his throat. This lock now develops into a battle of strength with the odds against your obtaining a submission. This is the time to discontinue the arm against neck struggle and apply your leg against your opponent. To do so, fall back bringing your left leg behind his head, using it to press

Fig. 102

forward whilst your left arm pulls back (Fig. 102). You should obtain an instant submission. Great care must be taken as it is usually difficult to judge the great strength brought to bear by the leg.

CHAPTER XV

LESSON 14

Hints on Bluff and the Continuity of Throws

As you become more experienced you will notice how in practice and particularly in contests two men of equal grade find it extremely difficult to throw each other. In fact the higher the grades, the fewer the throws, and the more contests end in draws or in locks and holds on the ground. Of course when a throw is effected it is always clean and fast and a pleasure to watch. There must be a sound reason for this—the skill of the men concerned is unquestioned and should they practise with a man of lower grade—even one grade lower—than themselves they are able to produce a series of throws in rapid succession. What then is the explanation for the stalemate when men of equal grade meet?

The reasons are several, usually they are also equal in experience and although they may favour very different styles, their ability is of the same level. If they hold high grades they are both relaxed in mind and body and therefore hard to throw at any time; if they are lower in grade they are probably both far too stiff and this fault in one is cancelled by the same fault in the other. Again they may have studied similar throws for approximately equal time and, in higher grades, the slightest movement from the opponent indicates the throw which is intended and the counter or avoidance to all appearances is made at the same time as the attack. In lower grades, strength and weight definitely effect the issue and decide contests but with Black Belts this is seldom so and this again aids in the "levelling up" process.

These even practices and contests affect judo exponents

in two possible ways; either one becomes discouraged at the lack of results or on the other hand you look for the reason behind your lack of success and settle down to seek and study methods of overcoming the difficulty. This is the stage at which the man adopting the latter attitude begins to make progress whilst the former stagnates. The intention of this lesson is to aid you to overcome these difficulties by suggesting methods, not as different moves and sequences to be learnt, but as ideas to be considered and probably built up to suit yourself and on which you can develop your own judo technique.

Very often when you attempt an Ankle Throw you find your opponent just managing to step over your left foot (the throws are presumed to be on the normal side—to the thrower's left—unless otherwise stated) and although he is off balance you cannot make him fall. At this point hold him in that "off balance" position and step to your right with your right foot making the same throw again; it will usually succeed. Never be afraid to attempt a throw twice, but ensure that you continue to hold your opponent off balance after the first effort.

Sometimes you find yourself completely unable to prevent your opponent escaping over your left foot from your Ankle Throws. There are two methods of dealing with this situation. Should your opponent jump over your left foot, a common way to dodge the throw, bluff him by moving your foot and body as if in a genuine attempt and as he jumps make the actual throw, catching his right ankle with the sole of your own foot when he is in the air. The resulting fall will be severe so make sure you check him. A second method is to make a sincere effort at your throw and if he escapes hold him off balance and replace your left foot on the mats, bringing your right hip and leg through to apply a Body Drop. You will find that your opponent has thrown all his weight on his right leg and is in a perfect position for that throw.

A popular combination of movements is to attack with an Ankle Throw on the reverse side but do not step back and to your left with your left foot—just draw your right hip back and place the sole of your right foot against the front of his left shin. As he transfers his weight to avoid this movement, turn to your left on the ball of your left foot and effect a Body Drop or a Sweeping Loin.

Very often you "get in" for a Hip Throw, but although your position seems reasonably correct, somehow you cannot make the throw. The reason for this is usually that your opponent has pushed his hips forward and bent his knees, thus shifting his position to one unsuitable for this particular move. The answer is to retain your hold round his waist with your right arm and keep up the pull to your left and your upward lift and at the same time lower your hips as much as possible, bending your knees. Now once more push your hips back into him and usually the throw will succeed. This is called a Resisting Hip Throw (Fig. 103).

For similar reasons you may find yourself unable to effect your Body Drop. This time you hold your opponent in the same position and lower your body still further. As you do so push your hips back into him and pull him close to your body with your arms. You should now be able to pull him forward over your right shoulder for a variation of the Shoulder Throw. This is another violent throw requiring care.

Fig. 103

Now for a Stomach Throw which combines well with the Major Outer Reaping.

Neither throw is effective against an opponent who shows good style, body upright and relaxed. Against such an opponent attacks such as Hip and Ankle throws are more effective, the actual throw itself blending into their movement for maximum effect. On the other hand you often meet the opponent who attempts to keep his feet well away from you to avoid being thrown but who also realises that he is thus leaving himself open for a Stomach Throw and is for that reason squatting down to prepare for it and is very difficult to bring down in this manner. To counter this you must manœuvre until you can catch him off-guard. Assume that you use your right foot to effect a Stomach Throw so that should you meet an adversary of this type, you should curve your body forward and bring up your right foot to his abdomen as if you were making a genuine attempt at the Stomach Throw. Instinctively he will resist, throwing his hips forward and his weight and balance back to his rear. You must immediately hold his balance in that position and placing your right foot back on the mats, slip in and past his right side with your left foot, bringing forward your right hip and leg to sweep his legs away in a Major Outer Reaping.

At this stage, he may make another effort to recover by thrusting his hips back and bringing his balance forward. Here you can turn to your left and should find you have sufficiently close contact to try a Hip Throw or if not a Sweeping Loin may be used.

Similarly you can deal with the man who keeps his balance back to avoid Ankle, Stomach or Hip Throws. This time bring your right leg up behind his right leg and begin to reap as for the Major Outer Reaping but this time do not step past him with your left foot, just come level with his right foot. As you commence this "reaping," your opponent naturally transfers his balance forward to escape and at this stage you can hold him in this position with his balance forward and bring your right foot up into his abdomen, curving your body forward to effect a Stomach Throw.

Very frequently you will attempt a Hip Throw only to be stopped by your opponent who places his left hand on your right hip as you begin to turn. Having done this, he attempts a counter Hip Throw only, in his turn, to be countered either by your hold on his belt or your own hand on his hip. Here we get a stalemate position, both of you working hard to effect your throw against strong defence. To persist in this position is extremely bad judo and ugly and tilts heavily against you in grading. Moreover it gives advantage to the stronger man. There are two methods of dealing with it; the first being the obvious one of ceasing your attempt and returning to a normal posture, the second is to hold your opponent in his curved position whilst you step back and to your left with your left foot, finally placing it on the mat to the left (his left) of your opponent's left foot. Now bring up your right thigh and leg and curve your opponent's body over them. Here a brisk flick of your hips will hurl him over your thigh to the mats. Your throw, which is a Sweeping Loin, is considerably aided by your opponent, who is still attempting to force himself in that direction for a Hip Throw.

In this lesson, as already stated, no effort has been made to lay down a series of moves designed to meet certain circumstances. What has been attempted is to make suggestions and give some examples on which you can build up your own contest attacks which will depend to a great extent on your favourite throws and movements. Groundwork holds and locks should also be built up in series, so that you fully understand the probable counter to each move and can follow up with a counter of your own. It should be borne in mind that the first effort must be a wholehearted attempt, otherwise you will not force your opponent into the posture you desire. Also your continuation move should not be made if your opponent's reaction is either insufficient or not as you had anticipated—in other words, if he has not broken his own balance for you.

The Use of the Legs in Groundwork

So far, only the more popular locks have been taught. Many others used are only variations of these and can be self-taught but there is one very important and usually neglected method of making your locks more powerful. Normally it is only shown to higher grades such as Brown or Black Belts because of the danger of sudden and vigorous application but by this stage readers should have learned to take care when applying locks and have sufficient control of themselves to apply them with due consideration to the person with whom they are practising.

The object is to use the leg to bring pressure to bear on the neck or joint on which the lock is being attempted but remember that it is not allowed by the rules of judo to use the leg against the neck to obtain a choke or strangle hold. The leg can be used against the back of your opponent's head or neck to increase the pressure exerted by your forearm or the jacket against the throat or carotid arteries. In many cases you will find that your body is not sufficiently supple to permit your leg to be brought into position and your attempt results in an attack of cramp. If this occurs, abandon your efforts until you have had more practice as, as well being painful to yourself, you are obviously without the required control to apply the lock without risk of injury to your partner.

The Winding Throws

Just as using the leg adds power to your ground attack, so does the use of the "Winding" technique add power and effectiveness to your throws. Similarly the danger of injuries to the person on whom you practise greatly

increases. The "Winding" versions of the throws usually
result in following your opponent to the ground much
to the detriment of his ribs and shoulder. If used to
defend yourself against attack this is to be encouraged as
you are unlikely to find your opponent able to regain his
feet, but when judo is practised as a sport a similar result
will be most unpopular with either your opponent or
club officials. For this reason great care must be taken
with the two throws which follow.

The Winding Body Drop Throw

As in the normal version of the throw described on
page 52, the left hip is taken back by moving your left foot
round and behind your right but this time the foot and hip

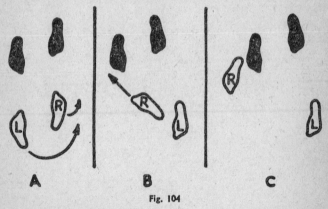

Fig. 104

are not taken round so far, your left foot being placed on
the mats only a little past your right (Fig. 104). As you withdraw and lower your left hip, you must of course break
your opponent's balance with the usual lift of your wrists
and pull of the left hand—the right hand pushing in the
direction of the pull. Once your opponent is off balance,
retain the left pull action of your left hand and release his
jacket with your right. Continuing to turn your body to

your left, bring your right arm over your opponent's
right shoulder and either
grip his right sleeve or hold
his belt or jacket in that
vicinity at his right side
(Fig. 105). With this grip
lift your opponent and pull
him to your left, assisting
the pull of your left arm
by dropping your right leg
back to trap his right (Fig.
105). As you carry on with
your turn to make your
throw, continue to lower
your hips by bending your
left knee. Take care as
your opponent will be
whipped off the mat sud-

Fig. 105

denly and take a very heavy fall. This action is often so
sudden that the thrower tends to
lose his own balance and fall as well.

The Winding Hip Throw

Fig. 106

Your opponent's balance is broken as for the Hip Throw on page
46, but this time you have to overcome your opponent's efforts to
hold you out and prevent your right
arm sliding round his waist to make
contact. This time give up this
attempt and instead push your hip
right out to your right to form a
fulcrum and slide your right arm
round his neck pulling his body
round you so that he is wound over
your right hip (Fig. 106). Continue

to turn and again you will find that you wind your opponent swiftly off his feet and over your hip to the mats.

The Shoulder Wheel

The last throw to be taught in this book is probably the most spectacular in judo but is, usually because of the nature of the throw, confined to small men. It can be brought off successfully by anyone on a taller opponent but it is safe to say that only a short man can find the opportunity to practise it sufficiently. It certainly can be included in judo's most difficult throws, if it is not the most difficult and for that reason it is very seldom seen outside displays. It must be emphasised at once that your opponent should not be lifted, the success of the throw depending on a powerful action of the hips. The opening occurs when your opponent pushes with his right arm preferably lifting as well. Immediately take your left leg and hip back so that both your feet are in line making a

Fig. 107

"T" with those of your opponent (Fig. 107). At the same time you must pull your opponent's left arm straight to his front —in the line of his push —and upwards, bending your knees and driving your right shoulder into him near his thigh—your head passing under his arm and your right side making close contact with his right side. Your right arm is brought between his legs and clasps his right leg round his thigh or knee. Your hips are now driven to your right making contact with your opponent's body between his knees and abdomen (Fig. 107). As you drive your hips to your right, your left arm continues its pull upwards and to your opponent's front whilst your right arm lifts. As a result of these combined efforts he is lifted from the mat and wheeled across your shoulders to take a heavy fall at your left side (Fig. 108).

Fig. 108.

This is a very heavy fall and in practice great care must be taken to check your opponent as, until he is familiar with this throw, the breakfall will cause considerable difficulty.

CHAPTER XVI

LESSON 15

Defence and Counters

Counters to some of these throws have been described already in order to make your judo training more interesting and to avoid the development of bad habits by the use of self-taught counters which may be basically unsound but effective against other beginners. The main point to remember is that in your efforts to avoid a throw you must not sacrifice your relaxed upright posture. To do so is to immobilise yourself and not only leave yourself open to successive attacks but place yourself in a position from which it is impossible to counter or develop your own attacks. These stiff defensive positions very easily become a habit which can be extremely difficult to shake off.

General Principles

Retain your relaxed and upright posture and make your defence by movements of your hips. Do not stop your opponent's movements but by moving your hips change your point of balance so that your opponent attacks your strength and enables you by assisting him to continue his movement to destroy his own balance. Counters cannot be made successfully by directly opposing your opponent's attack. If you do this, you stop his movement and therefore prevent your own counter.

Judo defence, and in fact judo generally can be classified in two categories:—

             (a) Positive.

             (b) Negative.

Considering (b) first, it is obvious that an experienced

man concentrating on avoiding being thrown can count on carrying out his plan successfully to a very great extent, but this is purely negative. This form of judo gives no chance of counter-attack or even making an attack— attack from a defensive posture is almost impossible. Similarly people adopting this method will never learn and will obtain no enjoyment from their sport. Finally this form of defence misses the very object of judo which is to throw your opponent in such a way that in a fight he would be disabled and unable to continue the attack.

Positive judo calls for a sound technique and relaxed posture, as well as a relaxed mind. It requires instant physical and mental reaction to your opponent's movements and seeks to avoid and overcome his attacks by the transfer of your balance, thus moving your body out of the line of his throw and enabling you to use his own movement to throw or counter-throw him. Against an opponent of your own grade it produces a thrilling exchange of move and counter-move, finally resulting in a clean and effortless throw. In self-defence it produces instinctive and effective defence and a devastating counter which will give the aggressor very little chance of making a second attack.

Whatever throw, lock, hold or form of judo you are practising at any time, always consider whether your methods are positive or negative and having done so, choose the former.

Counters to the Hip Group of Throws

In this chapter all throws are assumed to be made to the attacker's left—The Normal Side.

The Hip Throw group includes such throws as the Hip Throw, Sweeping Loin, Spring Hip, Winding Hip and for the purpose of this lesson, the Shoulder Throw. Strictly speaking the Shoulder Throw is a hand throw but the counter is best included with those to be described in this lesson.

To avoid these throws, as opposed to attempting a counter, very little more is required than to bend your knees and lower your body but this is negative judo at its worst and, as well as leaving you open to rear throws, it destroys any chance you may have of bringing off a throw of your own. A much better method is to check your opponent's turn with your hand against his right hip (Fig. 88 on page 135) and then move round him (to your right) so that you remain facing him. Another way which can be used when your opponent makes contact and begins to lift you with the throw is to lift your right

leg as much as possible and point your toes downwards (Fig. 109). You will then find that you cannot be thrown or, as an attempt is made to turn you off your opponent's hip, you can re-place your right foot on the mat and move round him in safety. Take care with this method as, if not successfully performed, it may actually assist the throw. Another alternative is to catch the right leg of your opponent's trousers with your right hand or his left trouser leg with your left hand and prevent him turn-

Fig. 109

ing you off his hip for the throw. Take care when adopting this method as an experienced man will throw himself and you will take a very heavy fall with him on top of you.

A similar method of avoiding a hip throw is to trap your opponent's right leg with your right foot (Fig. 110). Here again there is a danger of your opponent forcing the throw by pulling your right arm into him and throwing himself—and you—with most painful results to you, but with this method of avoiding the throw the danger is not as great.

Note

Fig. 110

These methods of avoiding the Hip Throw by trapping the opponent's leg with the foot or a grip on the trousers can be easily overcome if the "thrower" continues to hold his opponent in a Hip Throw position and then sharply swings his right leg forward, thus breaking the defensive grip. At this stage swing the leg back and throw with a Sweeping Loin Throw.

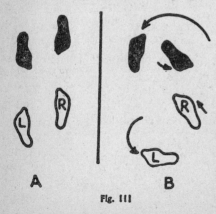

A

B

Fig. 111

The most simple counter to these throws is to catch your opponent with a downward turn of your wrists as he turns for his throw simultaneously turning to your left on the ball of your right foot and lowering your hip by bending your knees, particularly your left. This movement is very similar to the Drawing Ankle Throw performed to your left, your opponent's balance being broken with your arms as in that throw. The movement of the feet is shown in Fig. 111.

Another method of countering or avoiding throws of this group, especially Shoulder Throws, is to step to your left rear as the attack—to your right—is made (Fig. 111 on page 177, shows the foot movements), and at the same time his balance must be broken to his rear. The great difficulty in performing Shoulder Throws is to avoid, even if only for an instant, bending your body backwards and the counter takes advantage of this weakness. If the throw is good and your opponent retains his balance forward, you must attempt to break it backwards. In

either case, as you step to your left rear, place your left hand into the small of his back (Fig. 112), pushing forward and with your right hand and arm drive him round to your left in the direction of your movement. As his balance is broken to his rear, continue your turn to your left, taking your left leg and hip further and further round as necessary until he is thrown on to his back. If the momentum of the throw is not sufficient to obtain a contest point, follow to the ground as the position is ideal for a hold down or possibly a strangle from your opponent's rear.

Fig. 112.

An extremely effective but very violent and somewhat dangerous counter is what is generally called the "Rear Lift." In this counter you drive your hips into your opponent as he turns to obtain contact and break his balance to his rear. At the same time grip his belt with

your left hand and the right leg of his trousers at or
below the knee with your right and continue to bring your

Fig. 113

hips forward to maintain contact with his body, immediately lifting him with your hips (Fig. 113). As soon as you
lift him withdraw your left hip and the leg if necessary and
throw him on to his back at your left side. It is essential to
continue to turn to your left by withdrawing your left
hip as otherwise your body will be in the way, making a
throw impossible.

Finally there is a popular method of avoiding
attempted throws to your right which necessitate your
opponent having close contact. As he turns, attempting to
maintain contact, bring your right shoulder back sharply,
throwing back your arm thus breaking the contact on

Fig. 114

your right side and making the throw impossible. The best means of doing this is to draw your arm back and upwards as shown in Fig. 114.

CHAPTER XVII

LESSON 16

Useful Locks in Self-Defence

NOTE: These locks are forbidden in Judo

Leg Locks—General Notes

Leg locks are forbidden in judo because of the danger of serious injury to the knee. They can be classified into three groups similar to those of the arm lock.

(1) Locks applied against the bent leg.

(2) Locks applied against the straight leg.

(3) Locks applied to the muscles of the leg.

One lock in group (1) will be described and two which could fit into either groups (2) or (3).

These locks should be practised with great care especially when your opponent or partner rolls over to avoid them. They should never be applied with a jerk or with too much enthusiasm. They can of course be applied to either leg with either arm.

The Standing Leg Lock

Its main use is as a counter to a kick in self-defence but it is also true that most judo exponents leave themselves very open to it in contests and practice taking advantage of the ban against them. Your opponent's leg is caught with your left arm, the short boney edge of your forearm being pressed against the back of your opponent's leg at the lower part of the calf. His foot, toes upward is tucked under your arm-pit (Fig. 115). The lock is applied by lifting your forearm and lowering your body by bending the knees and pushing your hips forward. Watch that

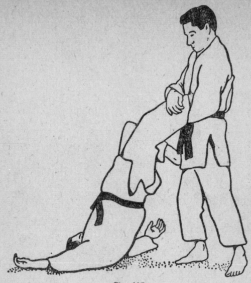

Fig. 115

you do not leave yourself open to a kick from your opponent's other foot.

When attempting this lock, keep the toes of the foot
under your arm pointed upwards.

Leg Lock on the Ground

This is similar to the Standing Leg Lock but is applied
when both your opponent and yourself are on the
ground. His foot is caught with your left arm and the
foot passed under your arm-pit, pressure being applied by
lifting your hips. Your left or right leg according to
which of your opponent's legs you are locking should
be passed across his body to hold him down. If this tends
to leave you open to a counter by a kick, place your leg
across his legs instead just about at the level of his knees.
Again keep his toes pointing upwards as you apply the
lock.

Lock Against a Bent Leg

This lock is usually applied against an opponent who lies on the ground with his back to you or rolls over possibly in an attempt to escape the lock just described.

Fig. 116

Immediately grip his leg with your hands and bend it backwards from his knee. As you do so place your own leg across the back of his knee so that it acts as a wedge (Fig. 116). Push his leg back until it presses against your own leg, obtaining the submission by gradually increasing the pressure.

Wrist Lock

This lock can be applied at

Fig. 117

any time you are able to grip your opponent's hand but its main use is probably against grips on the hair or clothing. Your opponent has grasped your left lapel with his right hand. Immediately grasp his hand with, preferably, both your own thumbs against the back of his hand and fingers against the palm—his fingers should be left upwards and the back of his hand towards you (Fig. 117). Keeping your body curved forward continue to press downward against the back of his hand until the intense pain caused by the lock makes your opponent submit.

Finger Lock

This lock is very similar to the Wrist Lock but this time you grasp your opponent's fingers and keep the palm of his hand towards you. Your thumbs should press against the front of his fingers between the lower joints with your fingers against the back of his hand. Curve your body forward pressing downward against his fingers which should be kept pointing upwards.

Leg Crush or Scissors

This is a very powerful lock and if applied by a strong person is capable of causing severe internal injury. The opportunity occurs when both contestants are on the ground. Your opponent is caught between your legs with

his body just above your knees. Your feet are immediately locked together (Fig. 118). Apply pressure against his body just below his ribs with your thighs but to avoid

Fig. 118

injury in practice, ensure that the pressure is applied steadily and is relaxed immediately your opponent submits.

SPEED IN JUDO

Although skill, relaxation, balance and smoothness of movement all play their part in Judo technique—and a very important part is played by each—there is one essential to success which I have not mentioned—that is speed. At first as you study Judo concentrate on general theory and devote all your efforts towards building up a good style, but once you are satisfied that your technique is sound you must try and obtain speed and still more speed. Take each throw in turn and try it slowly, stopping when you reach the stage when your opponent is just about to fall. Now try again faster—step back and try again, again and again about a dozen times. At this stage you will be feeling pretty tired so let your opponent have a turn on you and then try again yourself. Speed is essential to success and must be built up but never at the expense of smoothness of movement.

APPENDIX

EXTRACTS FROM THE
RULES GOVERNING JUDO CONTESTS

In order to standardise judo technique and ensure that unnecessarily dangerous moves are not attempted, the clubs of the British Judo Association have drawn up the following rules to be observed in contests. Various clubs make private amendments to these rules to suit local conditions such as small mat areas. To assist beginners some notes on these rules have been added.

1. A contest shall begin after the ceremonial bow when the opponents are in a standing position, and shall last 5 minutes or as arranged or until one contestant scores one point.

2. The winner of the contest shall be the individual who first secures one point except as provided for otherwise by Rules 14, 15, 17, 18. In the event of no points or equal points having been scored at the end of the specified period the Umpire may award the contest to the individual showing the best style or spirit or he may pronounce the contest a draw.

3. A throw, lock or hold shall each count one point.

4. A throw to be counted as a point must fulfil the following three conditions.
   (a) executed intentionally.
   (b) executed with certain impetus.
   (c) the opponent is thrown on to his back.

5. Should a contestant be successfully thrown according to Rule 4, it does not matter how quickly or cleverly he may change his position afterwards and so throw, hold or lock his opponent, the first thrower gains the point, not the second.

6. When a contestant is in a standing position and skilfully lifts his opponent shoulder high, in such a way that a dangerous throw could be executed, the Umpire shall stop the throw and award him a point before the actual throw is made.

7. Any technique which is applied outside the mat area shall not be recognised.

8. Groundwork begins when a throw has been unsuccessful and one or both of the contestants fall to the ground. A contestant must not remain on the ground when his opponent is up and waiting.

9. Should one contestant go to the ground more than three times other than through the intended employment of throwing technique, the Umpire(s) may award a penalty point against him, following a warning.

10. The following conditions are necessary for locks to be recognised:—
    (a) The signal of defeat given by one competitor,
    or
    (b) The effect recognised by the Umpire.

11. When a contestant admits his defeat under a lock, he shall call out or lightly tap the opponent or the mat twice or more with his hand or foot.

12. A hold is counted as a point when a contestant holds his opponent on the ground for thirty seconds without the use of a lock. The hold is considered to be broken when an opponent puts his arm or leg on the body of the holder in such a manner that a lock or disturbance of the hold may occur. The counting of the time for holding shall not be interrupted by the termination of the specified period of the contest.

13. When the contestants are interlocked on the ground so that in the opinion of the Umpire neither contestant can either extricate himself or gain any advantage over the other, the Umpire may order both contestants to resume standing positions.

14. Should a contestant be injured and as a result be unable to contest further, then the Umpire may decide the contest on the following lines:—
    (a) Should the injury be due to his own struggles or carelessness, then the injured man loses one point.
    (b) Should the injury be due to similar actions on the part of the opponent, then the injured man is awarded a point.
    (c) Should the cause be traced to the carelessness of both or neither contestant, or be unknown, then no point is awarded.
    (d) Should a contestant not wish to continue the contest as the result of a slight injury, then the Umpire shall exercise his judgment and decide the contest.

15. Should one contestant be taken ill during the contest and hence be unable to continue, then the Umpire shall act on Rule 14.

16. The following actions are barred:—
    (a) Throwing the opponent on his head, neck or shoulders.
    (b) Twisting or bending fingers, wrists, toes, jaw, head or spine.
    (c) Ankle locks, leg locks, kidney squeeze, pinching, nerve pressing or blows.
    (d) Pressing against the face.

(e) Pulling down the opponent for the purpose of beginning groundwork.
(f) Squeezing the head with legs or arms.
(g) Applying locks with a jerk.
(h) Gripping inside the sleeves or trousers.

17. In the case of any barred action on the part of any contestant, the Umpire may stop the contest according to his own judgment and award an adverse decision accordingly.

18. Should a contestant infringe any of these Rules, the Umpire may stop the contest and without regard to the score of points decide the contest against the defaulter.

19. **In all cases the decision of the Umpire shall be final.**

Notes on the Rules

Rule 4 (*a*).—A point is not awarded against a contestant who falls in attempting a throw unless an intended counter is performed against him.

Rule 10.—It is forbidden to pull an opponent to the ground with the intention of commencing groundwork.

Rule 11 (*b*).—The umpire can award a point if either contestant is in danger of injury as a result of refusing to submit.

In many clubs 'sacrifice' throws are forbidden owing to the danger of one man being thrown on or against other people who may be practising at the time. Sacrifice throws are those in which the attacker throws himself in order to obtain a point (e.g. a Stomach Throw).

ADVANCED JUDO

Readers who have worked carefully through this book, especially those fortunate enough to have a friend with whom to practise, will have a good idea of judo theory and the basic principles of the most popular throws, holds and locks. You will have reached the stage where a qualified instructor and varied and good opponents are essential to further progress and I strongly recommend you to join a Club where misinterpretations of the descriptions of movements can be ironed out and finer points described in detail.

Choice of your club should be made with care as, unfortunately, there are several unqualified, self-graded professional teachers operating clubs or schools for personal profit. Many of these have either nothing more than a knowledge of "unarmed combat" obtained in the Forces or only hold a low grade obtained at a recognised club. The beautifully designed certificates of grading issued by these "Teachers" are valueless. It is worth going to considerable inconvenience to practice at a good club and I will be very pleased to advise readers who contact me at *LONDON JUDO SOCIETY*, *32, St. Oswald's Place, Kennington Lane, London, S.E.11.*

To give ambitious judoka an idea of the organisation of a judo club a brief description and history of London Judo Society follows:—In some respects this club is superior to others and in some inferior, facilities depending on such items as the premises available and the grade and number of instructors.

LONDON JUDO SOCIETY

Situated at 32, St. Oswald's Place, Kennington Lane, London, S.E.11, only some 15 minutes away from some of London's main railway terminals, the Club's premises consist of three large halls, complete with showers and dressing rooms. The mat areas are amongst the largest in Britain and the upper hall is complete with a cafeteria. The club is open every day of the week. A large junior club operates at weekends for boys from the age of 10. It is the Headquarters of the Metropolitan Police Judo Club and the London Taxi Drivers Judo Club. Beginners classes commence at regular intervals, all the instructors holding Black Belts.

When the present premises were taken over in 1947, only the ground floor was available and this had been turned into an air-raid shelter by blocking windows and dividing the hall into several sections by the erection of blast walls. After constant pressure, the local Council were at last persuaded to put the hall back into reasonable condition and after weeks of decorating by the members the hall was officially opened in January, 1947. The upper hall was opened in January 1952. Most of Britain's leading experts took part in the opening ceremony.

Club teams take part regularly in International Interclub contests, having met teams from France, Holland and Germany and having visited all these countries in turn. The Club also competes in the Judo League of which it was a founder member as it was also of the British Judo Association. In the league its team meets most other leading Clubs. In 1952 high grade members of the Japanese Olympic Team visited the Club to teach judo enthusiasts from all over Britain who came to see them perform and to be taught by them.

All new members are expected to take a beginners' course unless they have previous experience, when they may apply for full membership at once. At the end of the beginners' course, grading contests are held and the beginners may apply for full membership of the club, which carries with it the right to practise in the upper hall with the higher graded members. Each course consists of a maximum of 16 beginners out of which about 4 or 5 usually win yellow belts, a very good effort. The remainder have never yet failed to gain promotion to white belt.

The Club welcomes visiting judoka to its premises to practise with its members and also visitors who would like to watch judo and make any enquiries, preferably on any Monday, Wednesday or Friday evening.

THE USE OF JAPANESE TERMS IN JUDO

Just as English words are used all over the world in football and French terms in fencing, so Japanese terms are used in judo and it is essential to know them if it is hoped to succeed in grading examinations.

Dispite this I have used the English names of the techniques described in this book only. This is because in many cases the book will be used by one or two people or small groups working on their own, and I hope it will simplify the instruction.

As later, readers must learn the Japanese terms, a list is included in this book in the hope that it will prove useful and instructive.

Brief Notes on Pronunciation

1. Consonants are pronounced as in English.
2. Vowels are pronounced as in Latin.
3. "E" is always pronounced "ay," e.g., NAGE is pronounced NA-GAY.
4. A "G" in the middle of the word is pronounced "NG" as in "SING" but otherwise is a hard sound as in "GOAL."
5. The letter "W" is usually silent as in "KWAI" pronounced "KI."

Ashiwaza	Technique of foot throws.
Atemi Waza	The art of attacking the body by striking, kicking, etc.
Butsukari (The word *Uchikami* is in more general use nowadays.	A method of practising the throws without actually throwing your partner.
Chugairi	The forward rolling Breakfall.
Dojo	The hall where judo is practised.
Fusegi	Defence.
Gyaku	Opposite
Gyaki Juji Jime	Reverse Cross Strangle.
Hadake Jime	Naked Strangle from Rear.
Harai Goshi	Sweeping Loin Throw.
Jigotai	Defensive posture.
Judogi	Judo costume.
Judoka	A judo exponent.
Ju-No-Kata	A demonstration of judo principles in slow motion.
Kaeshiwaza	The technique of counter-attack.
Kake	The attacking movement.
Kata	A prearranged series of movements performed for the purpose of demonstration.
Katsu	A method of resuscitation.
Koshiwaza	The art of making Hip and Loin throws.
Kuzushi	Breaking an opponent's balance.
Kami Shihogatame	Upper Four Quarters Hold Down.

Kata Juji Jime	..	Half Cross Strangle.
Kesagatame	..	Scarf Hold Down.
Nami Juji Jime	..	Normal Cross Strangle.
Nagawaza ..	..	The art of throwing.
Newaza ..	..	Groundwork.
Osae Komi Waza ..		The art of Holding.
Ogoshi ..	..	Floating Hip Throw.
Osoto Gari ..	..	Major Outer Reaping Throw.
Randori	..	Free practice.
Saika Tandem	..	Lower abdomen.
Shihan ..	...	A teacher.
Sutemi Waza	..	The Art of throwing from a lying position. (e.g., Stomach Throw.)
Shizen Tai ..	..	Normal standing position.
Shime Waza	..	The art of Strangulation.
Seoi Nage ..	..	Shoulder Throw.
Tachi Waza	..	The art of Throwing.
Tandem .:	..	The abdomen.
Te ..	..	A trick or method.
Tewaza	..	The art of making hand throws.
Tsuri Komi	..	The lift and pull on your opponent's jacket.
Tsukuri	..	The Breaking of Balance.
Tsugi Ashi ..	..	Movement sideways on the mat.
Tai Otoshi ..	..	The Body Drop Throw.
Ukemi ..	..	The art of Falling—"Breakfalls."
Ude Garami	..	"Figure 4"—Arm Lock.
Ude Hishigi	..	Straight Arm Lock.
Ushiro ..	..	Reverse as in Ushiro Kesa Gatame Reverse Scarf Holding
Waza ..	..	Technique—Art.
Yoko Shihogatame		"T" Hold Down (Side 4 Quarters).
Yudansha ..	..	A Dan Grade Holder (Black Belt).

PERSONAL NOTES

E. N. DOMINY. Profession: Civil Servant.

Hobbies: Judo, building and driving cars, all sports especially athletics. Ice-hockey for Civil Service.

Graded 1st Dan by K. Koizumi, 7th Dan.

Graded 2nd Dan by I. Hatta, 7th Dan of the Kodokwan, Tokyo.

Joint founder (with G. W. Chew) of London Judo Society in 1946.

Instructor to London Judo Society, London County Council, Leeds University, Northampton Judo Club, etc., etc.

Instructor on several National courses.

Hon. Secretary, London Judo Society.

Served several years on Executive Committee of the British Judo Association.

Display and Contest Secretary for the European Championships, London, October, 1953.

Vice-President of Kettering and Grimsby Judo Clubs.

President of Northampton, Spalding, Cleethorpes, and Eastbourne Judo Clubs.

British International v. Holland, 1949.

Reserve for Britain v. France, 1951.

Represented London Judo Society in Holland and France, and met Schill, champion of Germany, 1952, in London, and Unterburger, champion of Germany, 1951, in Cardiff.

Started judo in a German prison camp in 1943—later succeeded in escaping from Germany. Joined the Budokwai of which he was Hon. Treasurer and Team Captain.

Author of:—

Teach Yourself Self-defence
Teach Yourself Karate
Judo Basic Principles
Judo Throws and Counts
Judo—From Beginner to Black Belt
Judo—Contest Techniques
Camping at Home and Abroad

Editor of *Judo Review*.

Chairman of the Civil Service Judo Association.

INDEX

194